MELANI

MANAGING CONTENT DESIGN TEAMS

A Guide for Product and UX Leaders

Managing Content Design Teams: A Guide for Product and UX Leaders
Copyright © 2025 by Melanie Seibert

All rights reserved. No part of this book may be reproduced or transmitted in any form or by any means without written permission from the author.

ISBN: 9798296473370

Edited by Jen Mediano
Cover art by Anze Ban Virant - ABV atelier design

CONTENTS

Foreword v

1	Content Matters More. 1
2	Content-First Design 24
3	Hiring Content Designers. 49
4	Managing Content Designers 76
5	The Collaborative Design Sprint 86
6	Three Ways to Structure Your Content Design Team 96
7	Content Designers and AI 108

Acknowledgements 123

Index 125

About the Author 133

FOREWORD

Back in 1978, it's rumoured that programmer Jef Raskin at Apple began designing the UI for the Apple II by writing down the conversation he wanted the computer and the user to have. This is what we now refer to as content-first design.

It might have been a novel process then. But step forward half a century, and any content designer will confirm that, even now, we're still having to instill the notion that designing from a content lens is just as important (arguably more so) than from a visual one.

At the same time, the emergence of AI is welcomed, and exciting. There's no hiding the fact that good outcomes from AI start with good, structured content input—something content designers have been creating for years.

In fact, businesses with low content maturity are going to struggle without the skills they need to generate the quality of experience that users will (and already do) expect.

Investing in specialist skills, though, takes knowledge. It's not easy to know who to hire, and once they're in the business, how do you set content experts up for success?

So many content designers fail to thrive when a business hires them but hasn't considered how to adapt their process or provide the right support to actually get the best from them.

Grass roots advocacy will almost never work—there has to be top-down appreciation of the role that content plays, and how to bring a content focus into design teams.

It's no longer enough to think that content design is just copywriting, or a nice to have. If you care about the user experience, you need to care about content design. You need to care about using AI intentionally within your content and design processes—and using content design to create your AI products—to get the best outcomes.

If you're not sure where to start, start where you are, and take comfort in the fact that resources like this book can help you on your journey!

Rachel McConnell
Author of *Why You Need a Content Team* and *Leading Content Design*

CHAPTER 1
CONTENT MATTERS MORE

"Design is the rendering of intent."
—JARED SPOOL

As a manager on Citibank's operations team, Sanjay's[1] first order of business on August 12, 2020 was to review his team's work for the previous day.[2] His team's job was to process credits and debits to their clients' accounts, and Sanjay needed to ensure there were no discrepancies. But as he began to examine the transactions, he could tell something wasn't right.

The day before, Sanjay's team had received instructions to pay $7.8 million in interest on a loan taken out by Citibank's client Revlon. One of Sanjay's team members, Viraj, had entered the transfer into Oracle Flexcube, the application Citibank's operations team used for transfers like this. The Flexcube screen is shown in Figure 1-1.

---

[1] I've changed the names in this story to avoid damaging the reputations of victims of poorly designed software.

[2] Full details of this case can be found in the ruling of the U.S. District Court for the Southern District of New York: *In re Citibank Aug. 11, 2020 Wire Transfers*. https://storage.courtlistener.com/recap/gov.uscourts.nysd.542310/gov. uscourts. nysd.542310.243.0_2.pdf.

BDLL	Borrower LIBOR Drawdown Prod		Drawdown
001BDLL201480094		001BDLL201480094	
024462		REVLON CONSUMER PRODUCTS CORP	
Facility Name	REVLON TERM LOAN 2016		

GL Detail

Component	Internal GL	Overwrite default settlement instruction
COLLAT		
COMPINTSF		
DEFAUL		
DFLFTC		
FRONT		
FUND		
INTEREST		
PRINCIPAL	3003000023	✓

Figure 1-1. The Oracle Flexcube screen Viraj saw when he entered the Revlon interest payment on August 11, 2020.[3]

In Flexcube, the best way to make an interest payment like this was to transfer the entire loan amount, sending the principal to an internal Citibank account and the interest to an external lender account. When they looked at the Flexcube screen, the Citibank team saw that the "PRINCIPAL" field was checked and the internal account number entered correctly. To them, that signaled that Flexcube was to send the principal amount to the internal Citibank account. When Sanjay tried to proceed with the transaction, Flexcube flashed a warning:

> **Account used is Wire**
> Account and Funds will be sent out of the bank.
> Do you want to continue?
> Yes   No

---

[3] *Ibid*, 13.

This didn't raise any alarms, because while the principal was being sent to the internal account, the interest payment was going to the lenders. Sanjay clicked *Yes*, finalizing the transaction.

So, why was the internal Citibank account missing nearly a billion dollars? Could it have been caused by a simple computer bug?

Sanjay emailed Scott, the Citibank manager in Delaware who had initially requested the interest payment. "Can you please review and advise if this [issue] needs to be raised to tech[?]" Sanjay wrote.

Scott did review the transaction. Soon, his response came: "Oh my."

It was then that Sanjay, Viraj, and Scott discovered that Flexcube required entries in *two more fields* in order to send the principal amount to the internal account. By leaving those fields unchecked and empty, the team had inadvertently told Flexcube to send the entire principal amount—not just the interest—directly to the lenders.

A two-year legal battle ensued. Citibank asked Revlon's lenders to return the erroneous payment, and the bank got about $500 million back right away. But several lenders resisted. It would be two years before Citibank would reach an agreement with the Revlon lenders.[4] By that time, Citibank had paid an undisclosed amount in legal fees, and U.S. bank regulators had fined them $400 million for "longstanding deficiencies" in their risk management and other processes. In the wake of the ordeal, the Citibank CEO resigned.[5]

Most people who, like you and me, work on digital products do it because we care about the people who use those products. As product and UX people, we believe that, in an age when we need the help of

---

[4] "Citi, Revlon lenders reach deal over $500 mln accidental payment." Dec 16, 2022. *Reuters.* https://www.reuters.com/legal/citi-ends-litigation-with-revlon-lenders-over-500-mln-accidental-payment-2022-12-16/.

[5] Son, Hugh. "Why Citigroup's CEO is retiring earlier than expected, paving the way for the first woman to run a major U.S. bank." September 10, 2020. *CNBC.* https://www.cnbc.com/2020/09/10/why-michael-corbat-is-leaving-citigroup-paving-way-for-jane-fraser.html.

technology to do just about everything from paying the electric bill to applying to college, making software applications easier to use really improves people's lives. We want to be a part of that betterment. Life is difficult enough as it is. We want to do the opposite of what Flexcube did: we want to make people's lives less stressful, not more so.

Try to imagine what it felt like to be in Sanjay, Viraj, or Scott's shoes on August 12, 2020. What would it feel like to go home one evening believing you had just cost your employer nearly $900 million? How would you explain what happened to your spouse, parents, and friends? Would you worry about getting fired? Would you be able to eat or sleep? How would you feel when the media spread the story, publicly associating your name with such a costly blunder?

In court, Scott said that after Sanjay had discovered the mistake and alerted him, "I accepted that the mistake had not been caused by any sort of glitch but rather by human error, and that I was one of the humans responsible for the error."[6]

He's only half right: the Flexcube debacle *was* the result of human error, but Scott wasn't the human who had caused the error.

WHEN JARGON ATTACKS

Shortly after content designer Tracey Vantyghem began working for the software company Zipline, she discovered something interesting about their app.

Zipline, which makes software for retail companies, used the word "upperfield" to refer to regional managers who oversaw several store locations. Vantyghem suspected that users didn't understand what this word meant. She was right: by surveying users, she learned that only

---

[6] Dolmetsch, Chris; Doherty, Katherine; and Surane, Jenny. February 18, 2021. "How Citi gave away $900 mn by mistake." *Mint.* https://www.livemint.com/industry/banking/how-citi-gave-away-900-mn-by-mistake-11613666006947.html.

18% understood the term "upperfield." Worse, 72% of the app's business users felt the term was classist, with "upper" implying that managers were more important than individual contributors. Zipline had been offending almost three-quarters of its users without knowing it.

Recounting this story in her book *Strategic Content Design*, Erica Jorgensen explains that one of Zipline's first customers used the term, and it had stuck, becoming part of the company's standard vocabulary. "Perhaps it stuck because the content design team wasn't staffed at that point and not involved in the decision to use 'upperfield' on the website, in marketing materials, and so on."[7]

Zipline is not the only tech company to suffer the consequences of underestimating content design. In fact, all tech companies do this.

Satisficing, or why we eat bologna sandwiches

Everyone eats food. Most people eat 3-4 times a day. However, unless you're very busy, wealthy, or both, it may never occur to you to pay a personal chef to cook all your family's meals. This despite the fact that you know food is key to keeping you and your family alive. So, why don't you pay top dollar to optimize every eating experience?

Because humans satisfice. Satisficing means picking the first acceptable solution that presents itself.[8] It's lunchtime and your kids are hungry, so you satisfice by serving them a bologna sandwich. While a warm grain bowl with quinoa, roasted sweet potatoes, and lean chicken breast is objectively better, a bologna sandwich will make your kids happy, is inexpensive, and is easy to make. Regardless of how much healthier and tastier the grain bowl will be, the bologna sandwich wins.

---

[7] Erica Jorgensen. *Strategic Content Design: Tools and Research Techniques for Better UX*, 110.

[8] Simon, H. A. 1956. "Rational choice and the structure of the environment." *Psychological Review* 63, no. 2: 129–38. https://doi.org/10.1037/ h0042769.

Satisficing works well in everyday life. Your kids will likely grow up just fine eating bologna sandwiches instead of grain bowls most of the time, as long as you toss them enough fruits and vegetables now and then. This holds for other areas of life, too. Just as you don't hire a personal chef to make lunch for your family every day, you may not hire a personal trainer, a chauffeur, and a housekeeper to plan your workouts, drive you places, and clean your house, because you feel like you can do a good enough job at these tasks yourself. In fact, trying to optimize all these activities—hiring a chauffeur to give you the absolute best transportation experience and a chef to give you the most outstanding Tuesday lunch—would take so much time and energy (not to mention money) that it would totally stress you out.[9]

There's a time for satisficing. There's also a time for optimizing. Throwing together a sandwich works for lunch at home on a Tuesday. But if you're opening a gourmet French restaurant, you'd better hire a chef—a really good one.

Writing your own emails and texts is great. But if you're building products that rely on language to help thousands or millions of people do their job, pay their bills, or find a ride to work, you'd better hire an expert to do the writing.

Unfortunately, most organizations don't even know they're satisficing with their content until their product is live and their team has 50 engineers and 20 visual UX designers[10] on it. It's only then that they realize they've been serving the content equivalent of bologna sandwiches to users who expected a gourmet meal.

---

[9] Sarkis, Stephanie. August 4, 2019. "Why 'good enough' is excellent for your mental health." *Forbes*. https://www.forbes.com/sites/stephaniesarkis/2019/08/04/why-good-enough-is-excellent-for-your-mental-health/?sh=37a566071233.

[10] In this book, I'll distinguish content designers from their more visual design-oriented UX peers by using the term "visual designer" or "visual UX designer."

CONTENT IS CRITICAL TO YOUR PRODUCT'S SUCCESS

Let's switch to another food metaphor: content is the ice cream in the product design sundae. You can't have a design without content any more than you can have a sundae without ice cream. But in the beginning, content was treated more like a topping. (Imagine a sundae that was just a pile of sprinkles with little glops of ice cream on top. Sound appetizing?)

Teams created visual designs and then tried to add content at the end, glopping it on top. It didn't work. They found that they needed to add a paragraph where the design only allowed a headline, or vice versa. The content broke the design.

Organizations are still making this mistake. We need to stop. We must acknowledge that apps need words more than they need visuals. Language is the primary technology that people use to form and communicate ideas, and has been for thousands of years. It's like the operating system of our brains. Because it's wired into us, no technology will change language's role in thinking and communicating.

So, in order to be usable, a digital product must communicate with the people who use it. Rather than being purely visual, UX design is also necessarily linguistic and conversational. As Erika Hall writes in her book *Conversational Design*, "The way humans use language—easily, joyfully, sometimes painfully—should anchor the foundation of all interactions with digital systems."[11] In other words, content matters more than visuals.

In the tech world, however, most people still think of design as visual. To most people in tech, the "designer" is the person who picks the colors, fonts, and illustrations you see on the screen. The "designer" determines how much padding surrounds the text and the exact radius for the rounded corners on the buttons you click. The "designer" makes

---

[11] Hall, Erika. *Conversational Design*, 10.

a website, app, or digital experience pretty. But that's not the core of what design really is.

Content design (also called UX writing) is the practice that forms the core of design. The Nielsen Norman Group defines UX writing as "the practice of writing carefully considered information that addresses people's contexts, needs, and behaviors."[12] Sarah Winters, author of the book *Content Design*, writes that "Content design is answering a user need in the best way for the user to consume it."[13]

We can all agree that the way a product looks—including its typography, layout, and whitespace—is valuable. I worked for one company that made a purely aesthetic update to fonts and colors that, it estimated, would add millions per year to its bottom line. A polished visual aesthetic gives a product credibility and can increase its earning power, while poor or inconsistent visuals can signal a lack of trustworthiness, prompting users to flee.[14] But as valuable as the product's visual aesthetic is, its content is even more valuable.

Yes, *content design is more important to your product's success than visual design.* Consider the home screens for Indeed (Figure 1-2), Craigslist (Figure 1-3), and Google (Figure 1-4).

---

[12] Kaley, Anna. June 26, 2022. "UX writing: study guide." *Nielsen Norman Group.* https://www.nngroup.com/articles/ux-writing-study-guide/.

[13] Winters, Sarah. December 5, 2019. "What is content design?" *Content Design London.* https://contentdesign.london/blog/what-is- content-design.

[14] For example, when Dropbox redesigned its Plans page, conversion metrics suffered, with their designer Arlen McCluskey theorizing that the bold new color palette was the cause. See Verber, Ariel. May 8, 2018. "How Dropbox is making their rebranding work." *Muzli.* https://medium.muz.li/how-dropbox- is-making-their-rebranding-work-576171842a75.

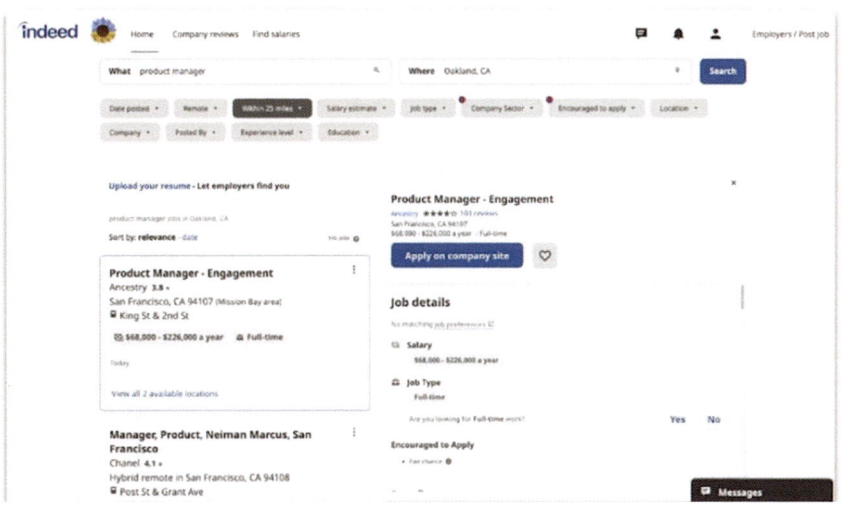

Figure 1-2. *Indeed.com (top) shows job listings matching your search query. Without the content (bottom), it's completely unusable.*

Content Matters More

Figure 1-3. Craigslist.com is very usable despite minimal illustrations, decoration, or other visual elements aside from text.

Figure 1-4. Google's homepage offers minimal visuals but extreme usability.

10 • Managing Content Design Teams

When I worked at Indeed, I surveyed 61 of my product manager, UX designer, and researcher teammates to find out how much value they got out of working with a content designer.[15]

When I asked them how working with a content designer affects the quality of their solutions, 69% of respondents gave a rating of 5, indicating that they deliver much higher quality with a content designer on the team than without.

Another 21.4% of respondents gave a rating of 4, indicating that working with a content designer helps them deliver solutions with somewhat higher quality. 6.9% (4 respondents) gave a neutral rating. No one said that working with a content designer detracts from the quality of their product (see Figure 1-5).

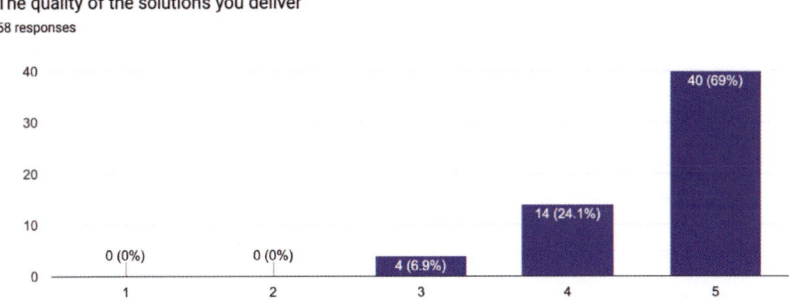

Figure 1-5. Responses to a question asking how working with a UX Content Designer affects the quality of solutions delivered. A rating of 5 means "much higher quality with Content Design," while a rating of 3 is neutral.

As for data from outside of Indeed, there are plenty of case studies that prove the value of content design. Here are just a few examples:

- Facebook's first content strategist, Sarah Cancilla, reported a content change that resulted in a 56% increase in traffic.[16]

---

[15] Melanie Seibert. February, 2024. "A survey of digital product teams reveals the value of content design." *Indeed.design*. https://indeed.design/article/a-survey-of-digital-product-teams-reveals-the-value-of-content-design/.

[16] Cancilla, Sarah. Foreword. In: Halvorson, Kristina. *Content Strategy for the Web*, xii.

- Sarah Winters, founder of Content Design London, reported a content change for the UK government that increased task completion by 88%.[17]
- When she was director of content design at Microsoft, Kylie Hansen reported that content design solved 44% of task failures and increased usability by 92%, as well as increasing active users and retention.[18]
- Expedia removed an unnecessary form field and gained $12 million in revenue.[19]

And those are just the results that can be measured in numbers. There are also other, harder to measure, ways that good content design improves your product.

CONTENT REFLECTS YOUR VALUES

Indeed makes digital products that help employers hire. LaFawn Davis, Indeed's Chief People & Sustainability Officer, points out that managers looking for "culture fit" can accidentally reinforce their biases when hiring, because the idea of culture fit camouflages our tendency to hire people like us.[20] Instead of looking for a candidate who's a culture fit, she

---

[17] Winters, Sarah. 2018. "Silo work is strangling user experience." *public.digital blog* (Winter). https://public.digital/signals/winter-2018/silo- working-is-strangling-user-experience.

[18] Swanson, Larry. November 11, 2019. "Kylie Hansen: building a content design team at Microsoft." *The Content Strategy Insights Podcast* 56. https://ellessmedia.com/csi/kylie-hansen/.

[19] Heath, Nick. November 1, 2010. "Expedia on how one extra data field can cost $12m." *ZDNET.* https://www.zdnet.com/article/expedia-on- how-one-extra-data-field-can-cost-12m/.

[20] LaFawn Davis. February 15, 2021. "Forget about culture fit—look for culture add." *LEAD with Indeed.* https://www.indeed.com/lead/culture- fit-vs-culture-add.

recommends that hiring managers look for a "culture add" by thinking about unique skills and experiences the candidate can bring to the team.

Now, imagine you're a content designer working on Indeed's digital hiring tools. Using the concept of "culture add" within the hiring tools, and explaining why it's important, could help managers minimize bias when hiring. Updating one term changes the entire framing of the value that the candidate brings to the company: instead of fitting in, they add something new. In this way, content design can help your users adopt new mental models and to act in accordance with your values.

Content makes products more accessible

Well designed content enables everyone to access and use your product. For example, visually impaired people use screen readers to navigate the web and apps. As part of the product development process, content designers should provide well written text descriptions for images and other visual elements that carry meaning, as doing so allows screen readers to convey those meanings to the visually impaired user. The descriptions will occupy an alt attribute in the HTML markup for images, or an aria-label attribute for other visual elements. Without these elements and a clear information hierarchy, visually impaired people can't use your product.

Content conveys your brand's personality

Have you ever seen a website that had bad grammar, missing punctuation, or an unhinged "personality"? Whenever I see content like this, it screams "SCAM" to me. I don't find it credible. I'd certainly never spend my money or share my sensitive information there.

Your product's content represents your brand to your users. Its language can take on the persona of a chipper, informal friend—perhaps a good choice for a travel app. Or it can sound like a wise expert to whom you'd be willing to entrust your money—a good choice for a bank. Whether you nail your brand personality in your content will determine whether users trust and use your product.

Content designers are critical to your product's success

Designing digital products requires many skills, typically including research, visual design, animation, writing, information architecture, project management, and more.

Why not just hire one person who can do all these tasks? Not only would a person like that be extremely rare, but it's also unreasonable to expect one person to do everything that well. Just as we wouldn't expect one engineer to take responsibility for front-end development, back-end development, and quality assurance testing, we shouldn't expect one designer to take responsibility for visual design, research, and content design. This is how you overwhelm and burn out designers.

And yet, tech companies routinely hire designers with no professional writing experience. Then they ask these designers to write—headlines, descriptions, field labels, error messages, calls to action, alt text for screen readers, and more. Leaders of these companies don't value content enough to pay a professional content designer for their expertise and dedicated time. This undervaluing of content ends up damaging the product and organization.

According to Sarah Winters, the reason content design isn't a respected skill is that everyone can write at some level. But she adds, "People who work with content designers generally change their minds pretty quickly."[21] As I found in the survey I cited above, once you've

---

[21] Winters, Sarah. December 5, 2019. "What is content design?" *Content Design London*. https://contentdesign.london/blog/what-is-content-design.

worked with a content designer, the benefits they bring to the team become clear.

THE ABILITY TO COMMUNICATE CLEARLY

I manage content designers, and I hire for writing ability. You might be thinking, "Hiring must be easy for you. Everyone can write." Think again. By assessing writing ability, I usually eliminate about 90% of applicants for content design jobs. And it's not because I'm judging their work by my own pet peeves or preferences. I'm looking for basic skills like:

- Grammar: do the subjects and verbs agree?
- Clarity: is the text logical and free of jargon?
- Relevance: is the writing free of verbal clutter? Does it get to the point?

To write good product copy, you need to be an expert at writing. The content designer might have a few characters to say something meaningful and unique. Remember the Flexcube warning modal? Flexcube only had a few words to warn the user he was making a billion-dollar mistake. They failed at that task, and it was a disaster for their client, Citibank.

THE ABILITY TO LAY A CONCEPTUAL FOUNDATION

Humans use language to structure our reality. Good content designers and UX writers necessarily do more than generate words. The Greek word for "word" is λόγος (logos), where we get the English word "logic." Writers are logic-makers. They create and align conceptual categories in ways that make sense of the world. That's important foundational work for your digital product.

Your product is made of ideas. And content design helps you forge those ideas—the conceptual building blocks of your product.

Indeed.com product director Audrey Santiago explained to me how collaborating with a content designer permanently changed the way her team worked. Her team had been working on an Indeed product that invites job candidates to speak with employers. "We learned quickly that the word 'interview' is understood differently by different employers. Some see an interview as a big commitment. Others think of it as just a quick call. So using this word affected the amount of risk they felt they were taking by enabling this feature."

Content design can help the team to choose another concept upon which to build the design, or it can help explain the concept of an interview in a clearer way, Audrey said. "Content designers are helping us determine how we structure and name these important concepts."[22]

A HOLISTIC PERSPECTIVE

Designers are often asked to focus on visual design for one feature at a time, making it difficult for them to keep the entire end-to-end user experience in view. And when a digital product is designed by one person with a limited perspective, it results in a complicated, broken user workflow.

This is where a content designer can really help. Indeed UX Designer Colin Robins told me that having a content design collaborator helps him think more holistically about the user's experience:

> For me, working with a content designer helps me understand: how can this design element apply, where should it apply, and how does it relate to other things?

---

[22] Seibert, "A survey of digital product teams reveals the value of content design." https://indeed.design/article/a-survey-of-digital-product-teams-reveals-the-value-of-content-design/.

> It's really useful to understand how information fits into this broader ecosystem.[23]

Similarly, Noni Hollands, Senior Design Manager at Atlassian, writes that,

> Because content designers need to consider the information experience, they are often looking more broadly across the end-to-end journey. They need to consider things like product discoverability, navigation, comprehension, ease of use, technical support, and troubleshooting on top of general UI designs and flows. Through this lens, they often uncover issues that other cross-functional peers do not see.[24]

THE ABILITY TO ENFORCE A CONSISTENT VOICE AND TONE

Content designers maintain the content standards for their products. Standards could include guidelines on how to use words like "interview." They could also include consistently applying the brand's voice and tone in the product. In her book *Strategic Writing for UX*, Torrey Podmajersky concisely defines voice and tone: "Voice is the consistent, recognizable choice of words across an entire experience. Tone is the variability in that voice from one part of the experience to another." As an example, she describes hearing her mother answer a phone call: "I can quickly tell by her tone whether the phone call

---

[23] ibid.
[24] Hollonds, Noni. June 27, 2021. "Noone says that they 'need' a content designer… until they get one." *Designing Atlassian*. https://medium.com/designing-atlassian/so-you-say-you-dont-need-a-content-designer-7bb94ea0704f/.

is from a stranger or a loved one—but I am never confused that it is my mother's voice."[25]

A content designer working on Oracle Flexcube, for example, would need to understand the voice that Oracle wants Flexcube to have, and the tone that it should take on in each interaction. This would help protect Oracle's brand and ensure that the software doesn't blame users for errors or needlessly irritate them by taking a humorous tone when they're having a serious problem.

To name a positive example, Slack is famous for their voice and tone. Their content design team works hard to delight the user and meet them with the right content at the right time, as when Slack's Huddle feature tells you that you look nice today (see Figure 1-6). This light remark can provide a little confidence boost in an otherwise potentially nerve-wracking moment—waiting for a work meeting to start.

Figure 1-6. Slack's Huddle feature displays a good grasp of voice and tone when it tells you that you look nice today.

---

[25] Podmajersky, Torrey. *Strategic Writing for UX*, 19.

COGNITIVE DIVERSITY

Harvard Business Review defines cognitive diversity as "differences in perspective or information processing styles."[26] This isn't the same thing as demographic diversity (differences in gender, race, or socioeconomic status, for example)—though demographic diversity can correlate with cognitive diversity. At its heart, cognitive diversity means having different ways of looking at the world, and different tools for solving problems.

According to research conducted by social scientist Scott Page, a cognitively diverse team has a better chance of creating a high-quality solution than a cognitively homogenous team does.[27] Staffing a UX team that includes content designers, UX designers, and researchers is a great first step toward gaining that cognitive diversity because it ensures that your team brings a diverse set of skills to their problem-solving process.

After studying design organizations, Professor Jeanne Liedtka from the University of Virginia reports that forming cognitively diverse teams is a significant predictor of five positive outcomes, including higher-quality solutions and better implementation.[28]

Today's software products are massively complex. They contain intricate, inter-related flows—series of screens that users must interact with, such as the checkout process in a shopping app—that depend on arcane internal systems. Updating them requires approval from multiple stakeholders, plus legal and accessibility reviewers. The process of designing or updating a flow like this and shepherding it through the necessary approvals, with all the negotiations that entails, is the definition of a complex problem.

---

[26] Reynolds, Allison and Lewis, David. March 30, 2017. "Teams solve problems faster when they're more cognitively diverse." *Harvard Business Review*. https://hbr.org/2017/03/teams-solve-problems-faster-when-theyre-more- cognitively-diverse.
[27] Page, Scott. *The Difference*, xxiii.
[28] Liedtka, Jeanne, November, 2019. "Investing in Innovation: Measuring the impact of Design Thinking."

You work on complex problems, so you need a diverse design team—one that includes content designers.

Content designers need time to work

Companies may hire one content designer at a time, creating a scenario where the trailblazing content design "team of one" is expected to support between 10 to 100 designers. The lone content designer is tempted to support all projects in tiny doses, often by setting up office hours or taking ad-hoc requests on Slack. This is better than nothing, but as Noni Hollonds explains, "the content designer will have an impact more broadly but they will be stretched so thin that their impact is very shallow. They'll be able to do a lot of the visible things but not operate strategically."[29] (A better approach is for the content designer to say no to some work assignments. Otherwise, he will have neither influence on the organization nor impact on the product.)

Instead of hiring too few content designers, companies should obviously hire enough content designers to do all the work that needs to get done. A good staffing practice is to hire a content designer to work with each visual designer—but certainly no fewer than one content designer per three visual designers.

And how should the design team engage with their new content designer? Early and often. In my survey of my co-workers at Indeed, when I asked them how their collaborations with content designers could improve, many volunteered that content designers needed to be involved in projects earlier. Similarly, the UX Content Collective's *2023 Content Design Industry & Salary Survey* reported that content designers identified their biggest problems as not being included in meetings and supporting

---

[29] Hollonds, https://medium.com/designing-atlassian/so-you-say-you-dont-need-a-content-designer-7bb94ea0704f/.

too many design projects.[30] Looks like there's a consensus—both content designers and their teammates say that content designers deliver more value when they're dedicated to a smaller number of projects.

Undervaluing content design damages the product and org

When companies don't hire enough content designers, or they don't give them enough time to focus on one product, the result is vague, jargon-filled interfaces like the one that Flexcube showed to Sanjay and his team. Let's look at it again:

> *Account used is Wire*
> *Account and Funds will be sent out of the bank.*
> *Do you want to continue?*
> *Yes   No*

This message does nothing to help the user.

- "Account used is Wire" doesn't make sense. In the Flexcube screen (see Figure 1-1), there's no "WIRE" account type.
- "Account and Funds will be sent out of the bank." That doesn't sound right. How is an account sent out of the bank?
- The message doesn't explain which accounts the funds will be sent to.
- How much is being "sent out of the bank"? And how much stays inside the bank?

---

[30] Szymanski, Katie. April 27, 2023. "Webinar recap: The 2023 content design & salary survey report." *UX Content Collective.* https://uxcontent.com/webinar-recap-the-2023-content-design-salary-survey-report/.

No amount of visual design expertise can fix these problems. Flexcube was a catastrophic failure of content design.

Understanding why content design is undervalued can help us start to value it properly. So, why doesn't your organization put content at the center of its design process? The answer to that question lies in your company's origin story.

A HISTORY OF EVERY TECH COMPANY EVER

Here's how tech companies start: a software engineer, or a group of them, creates a product. They're fortunate enough to find product-market fit. People want to pay money for a thing that the engineers used their coding skills to create! It's very exciting.

Now they have a company. And it just so happens that, since the product that brings in money is something that the engineers made with their coding skills, the company is focused around engineering.

It makes sense, right? Engineering is the practice that enabled people to create this product, and this company, out of nothing.

Pretty soon, a few things happen:

- The engineers realize they aren't that great at designing interfaces, or they don't want to spend their time designing.
- They hire a visual designer.
- They value the visual designer as a specialist who "makes things look nice," but not as a strategic thinker. As a result, the designer doesn't have much influence over staffing, organizing work, or the product roadmap.

It's still an engineering-focused company, so when leadership thinks about staffing and organizing the work, they prioritize engineering.

But over time, as the design work grows, the design team does too. They grow in numbers, as well as influence. As they begin to have a more informed point of view on the product strategy and come up with more strategic ideas, they may even begin to influence the business and the product at a deeper level. It's awesome.

Then a few more things happen:

- The visual designers realize they aren't that great at writing content for the software's user interface, or they don't want to spend their time writing.
- They hire a content designer.
- They value the content designer as a specialist who "makes things sounds good," but not as a strategic thinker. As a result, the content designer doesn't have much influence over staffing, organizing work, or the product roadmap.

This pattern plays out in tech companies over and over. Why? Because what typically prompted that little engineering team to hire its first visual designer was the feeling that they needed help making the product look a certain way. That's why they didn't hire a content designer first. They hired a visual designer to create mockups.

It's time to reject this visual-first mindset. It's time to recognize that content matters more than visuals. Your digital product is worthless if it looks good but no one can understand what they're supposed to do with it. Your product delivers more value as a way to communicate with users than as a visual artifact.

Prioritizing visual design over content is a holdover from the early days of tech, the result of a startup's first impulse being to make the product look better. In reality, content design and visual design should never be separated. Because content design can deliver more business value than visual design, each product team should have at least one dedicated content designer.

Now that you understand why it's important to include a content designer on your team, let's take a look at what that person will actually do day-to-day—the content-first design process.

CHAPTER 2
CONTENT-FIRST DESIGN

"Writing is designing."
—**MICHAEL METTS AND ANDY WELFLE**

I once worked as a content strategist on an agency team that was redesigning a hotel website. Our team included lots of skilled designers, engineers, and project managers, but just one writer. The client's in-house subject matter expert was the only person knowledgeable enough to write the website content himself. And he was swamped.

The designers, who knew how important content was to the design process, politely asked whether the writer would be able to deliver content before they started designing the site. No, he said. He was just too busy. The designers bravely soldiered on. They tried creating a design, but it wasn't right. They didn't know what they were designing, because they had no content. Was the page a single long-form text block? Did it have illustrations? A table? Or did it have several shorter text blocks with photos? Without content, they had no idea what to design.

Maybe you've been in this situation yourself. Maybe you were the stakeholder asking designers to create a website or product without content because you thought, "we can fill in the content after we design it." Or maybe you were the designer who tried to churn out screens and got frustrated because you had no way of knowing what your designs were supposed to say to users. Or maybe you were the sole writer buried under a mountain of work, dimly aware of the digital project churning in agony just outside your periphery.

If you've been any of these people, you learned a valuable lesson: design without content is impossible, because content is the product.

In this chapter, you'll learn a better way of working. We'll examine a content-first product design process. While there are numerous methods for "doing content design," this process has yielded success for my teams in the past. The process follows these four basic steps:

1. Mapping ideas
2. Drafting the conversation
3. Writing the content
4. Testing the content

You may be a UX manager, design director, or product manager. Or you could be a content designer or content design manager yourself. If you're not the one directly responsible for the content design, understanding this process will make you a much better partner or manager to the content designer on your team. And if you are responsible for the content design, understanding how to design content-first will help you create better products.

Mapping ideas

Ideas precede visual design. Successful design teams use one of a number of methods to map out the ideas that underpin their product's experience. That's because mapping ideas—based on user research—is a powerful way to start the design process, conferring a bunch of benefits:

- *It helps you to clearly define your concepts.* When I worked at Indeed, we had many conversations to define a job candidate. In order to get all the teams to agree on a clear definition, content designers ran a mapping exercise. In this exercise, we listed each stage of the hiring process and the terms that our products for employers and job seekers used to refer to candidates at each stage (see Figure 2-1). That enabled us to clarify that a candidate becomes an applicant only when they apply for a job, which helped us use terms consistently and coherently throughout our interfaces.

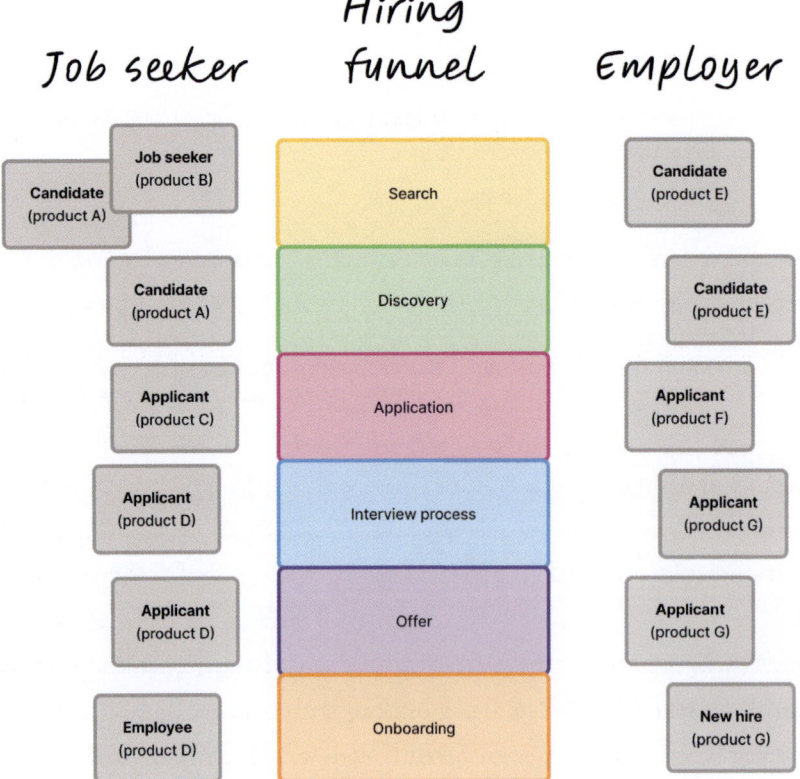

Figure 2-1. A simplified model of the candidate mapping exercise. Content designers worked together to audit products used in various stages of the hiring funnel, and when they found a word that referred to a candidate, they wrote it on a gray sticky note. We found that candidates were consistently called "applicants" from the application phase to onboarding.

- *It lets you structure your product in ways that make sense.* Once you've defined your concepts, mapping them helps you see which ideas are most important to users. Then you can put those important ideas front and center, using secondary attributes to explain them. For example, a financial services company might consider an account to be a primary concept, with attributes like name, address, and balance attached to it.
- *It helps you design the right actions, in the right order.* Digital products should inspire users to take action. To do that, they must be designed around the right objects (or concepts), because you need to know what things your user is acting on. Clarify which actions should be allowed to affect which objects. For example, if you're working on a social media tool, can a user comment on a post? Can they like and share it? Can they subscribe to a post? Understanding the actions and objects in your product helps you understand what steps users can take to reach their goals.

Object-Oriented UX:
A Method for Mapping Ideas

The most powerful idea-mapping method I've seen is Sophia Prater's method, called Object-Oriented UX (OOUX).[1] We won't do a deep dive on this method here,[2] because just a basic understanding will help your team immensely.

Prater's method hinges on answering four key questions:[3]

1. What objects make up the user's mental model?
2. What are those objects' relationships to each other?

---

[1] Learn more at the OOUX website: https://www.ooux.com/.

[2] If you're hungry to learn more, dig into Prater's course: https://www.ooux.com/foundations.

[3] Prater, Sophia. "The UX Level-Up." https://www.ooux.com/uxlevelup.

3. What calls to action can users perform on those objects?
4. What attributes do the objects have?

The acronym "ORCA", which stands for Objects, Relationships, Calls to action, Attributes, summarizes these questions.

Objects

I used to think that actions—that is, verbs—were the primary building blocks of design. But before you can enable a user to take action, you have to present them with things (objects) to act on. That's just how we navigate the real world, so it's how we need to navigate the digital world, too. And it's why a basic tenet of OOUX is that people think in objects—in other words, nouns.[4]

As an example, let's look at the Virginia Department of Motor Vehicles (DMV) website that I once perused with my teens (see Figure 2-2).

Figure 2-2. The Virginia DMV's website is organized around nouns.

Where would you go if you were a teenager looking to get your first learner's permit? Probably *Licenses & IDs*, right? That makes sense, and it turns out, it's the right answer. If the navigation used verbs instead, like Apply, you wouldn't know whether you were starting the process of applying for your first permit, a Commercial Driver's License for a semi truck, or a business license.

---

[4] Prater, Sophia. May, 2017. "The Object-Oriented User." https://www.ooux.com/resources/the-object-oriented-user.

28 • Managing Content Design Teams

In order to forage for the nouns that are relevant to your product, Prater recommends looking at user interview transcripts, as well as transcripts of customer service calls, user manuals, your marketing website—any content that pertains to your product. You can even forage for nouns on your competitor's website! Invite your team to help, and comb through these materials, pulling out the nouns that seem the most relevant. You'll probably be able to consolidate them, too. For example, if the team working on the Virginia DMV website foraged for nouns, they could probably combine "permits" and "licenses" since they're so similar. When you find similar terms, consult your user research to determine which term people use most often, and focus on that term in your product.

Relationships

Now that you've collected the nouns related to your product, you can map the relationships between them using a Nested-Object Matrix (NOM). You can do this collaboratively with your team, either on a real whiteboard with sticky notes, or on a digital whiteboard.

Making a NOM is simple. Once you've identified your nouns and consolidated them into the most important objects, list the nouns across the top, and then again down the left side. If we assume that the DMV recognizes licenses, vehicles, businesses, and people as important objects in its system, perhaps an early NOM for the DMV website might have started out looking like Figure 2-3.

	License	Vehicle	Business	Person
License				
Vehicle				
Business				
Person				

Figure 2-3. A blank Nested-Object Matrix for the Virginia DMV website.

Next, work through each cell, thinking about the relationship between the object at the head of the column and the object at the head of the row. For example, considering the column for Person, you might ask:

1. How many licenses can a person have? What are the types of licenses?
2. How many vehicles can a person have? Are there other ways a person can relate to a vehicle than ownership, such as renting a vehicle, or as a past owner in a vehicle record?
3. How many businesses can a person be related to, and what are those relationships?
4. Do relationships between people exist in the DMV system? For example, does a vehicle buyer necessitate the existence of a seller? Do children with an ID card or learner's permit need to be associated with an adult?

As you work through the matrix, you can see how this method causes you to think on a deeper level about the objects and the connections among them, which helps you to:

1. *Define your terms.* For example, can many people have the same license? Well, multiple people can have the same *type* of license (such as a learner's permit), but only one person can own a specific *instance* of a license. Clarifying that you're using the NOM to describe the license instance focuses the discussion on that object.
2. *Design the navigation.* If you're designing a DMV portal, and you determine that a business can have permits, you probably want to make sure that a user can click into those permits from the business's account, and conversely, access the business profile from the permit's detail page.

We've learned so much, and we haven't even opened Figma yet! Take a look at the completed NOM in Figure 2-4.

	License	Vehicle	Business	Person
License	n/a	n/a	Has 0 to many hauling permits	Has 0 to many driving permits
Vehicle	n/a	n/a	Owns 1 to many vehicles	Has 0 to many Vehicles
Business	Held by 1 Business (or Person)	Owned by 0 or 1 Business	n/a	Owns 0 to many Businesses
Person	Held by 1 Person (or Business)	Owned by 1 to many People	Owned by 1 to many People	Seller has 1 to many Buyers / Buyer has 1 to many Sellers

Figure 2-4. A completed Nested-Object Matrix for the Virginia DMV website.

Of course, this is just a snapshot; there are lots of details we haven't captured here. The types of licenses, businesses, vehicles, and people may each require a column of their own. And there are undoubtedly more objects we could map. The completed DMV NOM would be extremely large and detailed. The important thing is to align the team on the key concepts and relationships you need to represent, before you design.

Calls to action (CTAs)

Next, we want to identify the actions the user can take on each object in the system. To do this, we need to cross-reference the objects in the system against each user type we have. For example, two user types for the Virginia DMV website may be an individual and a business. List these in a CTA Matrix with objects across the top and user roles down the left side. Go down each column, asking, "What actions can this user take on this object?" (see Figure 2-5).

	License	Vehicle
Individual	Apply Pay fee Transfer from another state Renew	Title Register Buy/sell
Business	Apply (hauling permit, commercial license) Pay fee	Hold lien Register fleet Buy/sell

Figure 2-5. A CTA Matrix for the Virginia DMV website.

As with the previous exercises, interesting questions will emerge:

- When it comes to a hauling permit or commercial license required to drive in a professional capacity, is it held by the individual driver or the business?
- If it's the individual, what happens when the licensed person leaves the business; does the license go with them?
- Can a business buy or sell a vehicle just like an individual? What's different about the purchase process when you're a business?

Asking these questions up front will help you design a more robust website or app.

Attributes

Every object has attributes that describe it. Prater encourages us to think about two primary types of attributes:

- *Core content*: This is the data that makes one instance distinct from other instances of the same object. For example, a Business has a name, as does a Person. In the DMV's digital system, a Person may also have a photo.

- *Metadata*: This is information you could use to sort and filter objects in a system. It's also data that could be shared by multiple objects. For example, several individual Licenses could share an expiration date, and you could imagine a DMV employee sorting Licenses by expiration date in order to send notices to drivers. That makes the expiration date a type of metadata.

For each object in your system, list the core content and metadata you think you'll need to design for. Figure 2-6 shows a brief example from the DMV.

	License	**Vehicle**	**Business**	**Person**
Core content	License number	VIN License plate	Name Address	Name Address
Metadata	Type (learner's, driver, hauling, commercial) Date issued Expiration date	Type (sedan, truck, motorcycle) Color Weight	Type (freight, dealer, bank)	Date of birth Organ donor (Y/N)

Figure 2-6. Attributes for the Virginia DMV website

The Object Map: Putting it all together

Now that you've mapped your objects, relationships, and attributes, you can put them all together, creating an Object Map, as in Figure 3-7. (You can keep the CTAs on their own separate map.)

Content-First Design • 33

Permit	Vehicle	Business	Person
Held by 1 Person (or Business)	Owned by 0 or 1 Business	Has 0 to many hauling Permits	Has 0 to many driving Permits
Permit number	Owned by 0 to many People	Owns 1 to many Vehicles	Owns 0 to many Vehicles
Type (learner's, hauling, commercial)	VIN	Owned by 1 to many People	Owns 0 to many Businesses
Date issued	License plate	Name	Name
Expiration date	Type (truck, sedan, motorcycle)	Address	Address
	Color	Type (freight, car dealer, bank)	Date of birth
	Weight		Organ donor (Y/N)

Figure 2-7. An Object Map for the DMV website.

Keep the Object Map as a reference when you're designing. It's a visual representation of your user's mental model. Showing these assumptions about how your user thinks allows you to share your ideas with stakeholders and get feedback, making the foundational concepts of your design even stronger.

For example, if a Customer Support Lead looks at your Object Map and clarifies that, actually, a Business can't own a License, that's great to know. It also brings up more questions: do you need to attach the License to a Person, and the Person to a Business? If so, that's valuable information to have at this early stage. It's so much better to learn this now than after you've polished the final design!

Although this DMV Object Map is basic and simple, real-world Object Maps can be as detailed and messy as they need to be. Annotate them. Move things around. Make them serve your team.

Drafting the conversation

Put the Object Map aside for a minute—but don't put it too far away. Now that you've diagrammed the objects that will appear in your design, you can start creating another foundational piece: the conversations that will give narrative structure to your design. And when you're done, you can pull out your Object Map to make sure your conversations are describing the objects accurately.

In the 2015 article "Content-first Design,"[5] Steph Hay refers to content as "the conversation." Conceiving of product content this way causes the design team to ask themselves what the user would say to the product, and what the product would say to the user. It results in a more usable experience, as Erika Hall explains in her book *Conversational Design*:

---

[5] Hay, Steph. April 29, 2015. "Content-First Design." *A List Apart*. https://alistapart.com/blog/post/content-first-design/.

Most advice on 'writing for the web' or 'creating content' starts from the presumption that we are 'writing,' just for a different medium. But when we approach communication as an assembly of pieces of content rather than an interaction, customers who might have been expecting a conversation end up feeling like they've been handed a manual instead… Software is on a path to participating in our culture as a peer. So, it should behave like a person…[6]

Drawing inspiration from video games like Animal Crossing, Hay explains a new, conversational type of design process for a website project she was working on:

> …we facilitated discussions around how well the content seemed to be meeting audience expectations by asking those stakeholders, "What are the top questions your audiences ask? What are their top complaints?"

Hay's team then rewrote the website's most popular content while constantly asking "How would someone get here?" and "Where would someone go next?" in order to restructure the entire flow. The team wrote the website content in a Google Doc before they ever designed a pixel.

I've used this content-first method with great results. Your team can, too.

Using talk bubbles to draft the conversation

In 2018, I worked on an agency team redesigning the homepage for a bank. The first thing we wanted was research about the bank's intended

---

[6] Hall, Erika. *Conversational Design*, 19.

audience.[7] Fortunately, we had plenty of it: the bank's team supplied us with lots of data on their users, and our own researchers had already interviewed real users, created personas[8], and curated lots of details about what users needed and wanted. Understanding this research was crucial to the design process. Armed with this data, we were ready to begin thinking about initial designs. To get started facilitating the discussion about audience expectations, we used a simple method called talk bubbles.[9]

During the kickoff meeting at the client's office, we set aside an hour or so to start drafting conversations. I had brought several pages showing two columns of text bubbles: one column was for the bank homepage, and the other was for one of the bank's target personas. I handed a page to each client stakeholder and assigned each of them a persona. Then I asked each stakeholder to take 20-30 minutes to draft a conversation between that persona and the bank homepage. They each came up with a little conversation.

If you did that same exercise with the Virginia DMV team, you might end up with something like Figure 2-8.

---

[7] You can't do product design without a research process, and there is a constellation of research methods you can choose. If you're not familiar with them, read *Just Enough Research* by Erika Hall, *Don't Make Me Think* by Steve Krug, or *Continuous Discovery Habits* by Teresa Torres.

[8] For more context on personas, see Harley, Aurora: "Personas Make Users Memorable for Product Team Members." https://www.nngroup.com/articles/persona/.

[9] What follows is a modified version of the Talk Bubbles method created by Mave Houston for the Capital One design team.

Content-First Design • 37

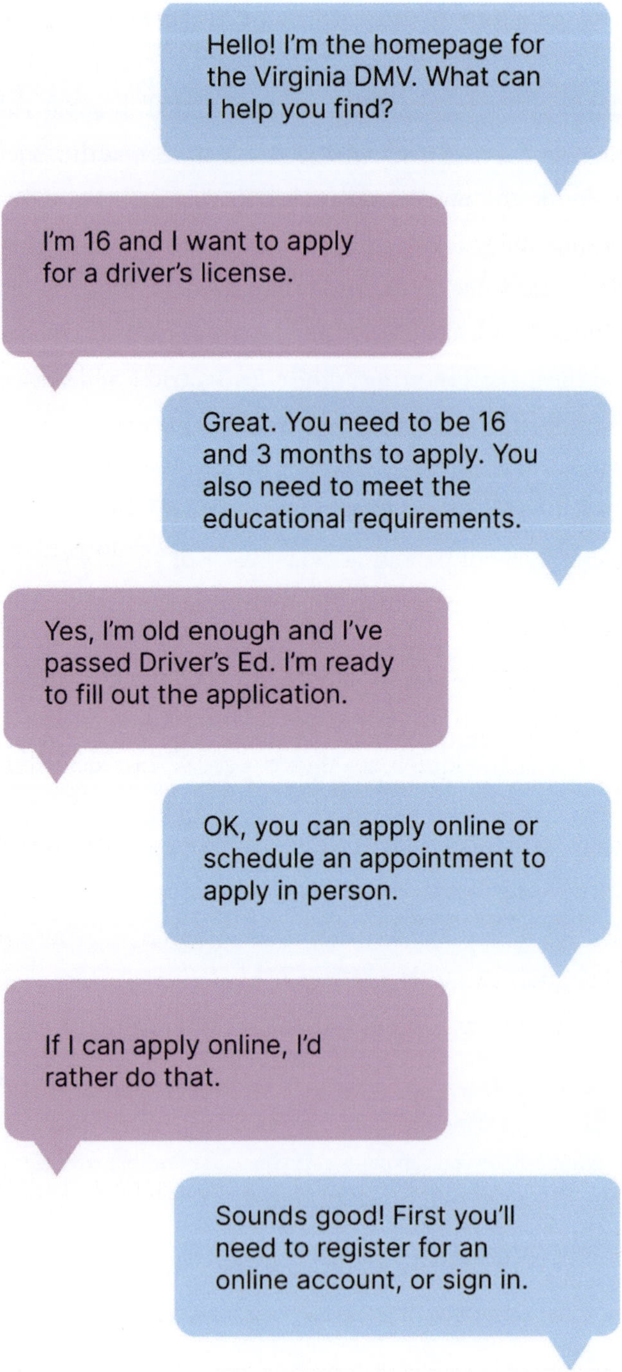

> Hello! I'm the homepage for the Virginia DMV. What can I help you find?

> I'm 16 and I want to apply for a driver's license.

> Great. You need to be 16 and 3 months to apply. You also need to meet the educational requirements.

> Yes, I'm old enough and I've passed Driver's Ed. I'm ready to fill out the application.

> OK, you can apply online or schedule an appointment to apply in person.

> If I can apply online, I'd rather do that.

> Sounds good! First you'll need to register for an online account, or sign in.

Figure 2-8. An example of a conversation drafted using talk bubbles.

In the example above, the conversation gives you good direction about what content to include on the homepage. It tells you that the persona—the teen driver, in this case—needs to see a few important things on the DMV website—and because these are the first things the user asks for, the easier they are to find, the better.

1. First, the user wants to know the requirements to apply for a driver's license.
2. Second, they want to know the ways they can apply (online and in person).
3. Third, they want to start their online application.

Designing the conversation is likely to give you more valuable information that you can feed back into your OOUX artifacts. For example, the conversation above names objects you hadn't mapped yet, like applications, educational requirements, and appointments. It also raises a relationship question: how do licenses relate to each other? Are some licenses (like a learner's permit) prerequisites to others? If so, you should note that in the Object Map. Keep iterating on the conversation and the Object Map until you understand the domain that's in scope for your project.

As you begin to write the content, you'll use the talk bubbles conversation as an outline, and refer both to the conversations and your Object Map to make sure you're including the important ideas and correctly describing how they relate to each other. For example, the DMV Object Map tells you that each person can have zero or more licenses, and that the person's metadata includes their name, address, and organ donation status. When you start to design the online driver's license application, you'll want to include these attributes as questions in that form.

Although it looks like something out of a comic book, talk bubbles are a powerful way to begin a content-first design process. Instead of jumping to a solution by envisioning boxes on a screen, you consult real data about users, then use that data to take a mental walk in their shoes. This helps you and your team to both feel empathy for each user's situation—which is crucial to designing usable experiences—and to lay the foundation for the website's task flows.

You can use the talk bubbles method with your stakeholders or with your design team members. Anyone who either talks to users regularly (think Sales and Customer Service) or studies them (like Product, Marketing, or User Research) is a good candidate to participate. The important thing is that your participants: 1) care about your users, and 2) understand your users.

Don't worry about getting the conversation perfect or covering every user need at this stage. You're just going to use these conversations to design a low-fidelity experience to build from. Later, you'll get user feedback on the content to make sure it includes everything the user needs.

Now that you have your updated Object Map and a few persona-based conversations to draw from, you can start drafting the product's content.

Writing the first draft

After reviewing the talk bubbles conversations, the next step is for the content designer to open a document in Google Docs (or Microsoft Word, or the word processing program of their choice) and start to write. Keeping the conversation drafts and Object Map in mind and referring back to them while writing the UI copy helps to ensure that the content meets the user's expectations for what they'll find and directs them where they want to go.

While writing the copy can be a group activity, I find that it's helpful to come into working sessions with some initial ideas the group can build on. A good approach is for the content designer to create an initial draft, then schedule a working session soon after to talk through the draft with the UX researcher and designer, and incorporate their input. This approach strikes a good balance between giving each team member time to think, and getting the benefit of many brains working on the problem. Different team members may remember different details from the conversations, and might offer alternative ideas how to order or lay out the information.

Steph Hay calls this document a content workbook.[10] Figure 2-9 shows what a content workbook might look like for the DMV example above.

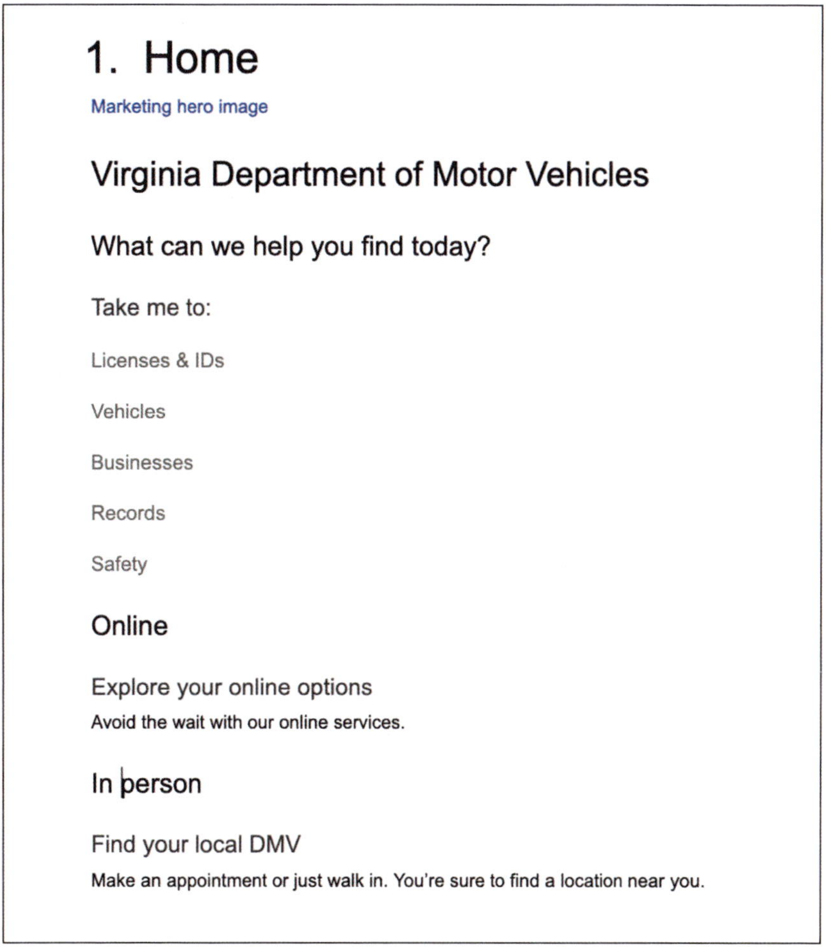

1. Home
Marketing hero image

Virginia Department of Motor Vehicles

What can we help you find today?

Take me to:

Licenses & IDs

Vehicles

Businesses

Records

Safety

Online

Explore your online options
Avoid the wait with our online services.

In person

Find your local DMV
Make an appointment or just walk in. You're sure to find a location near you.

Figure 2-9. An example of a copy workbook for the Virginia DMV homepage.

---

[10] As an example, she provides her own content workbook, "Content, IA, and Flow for the *Annie E. Casey Website*." https://docs.google.com/document/d/1S1U-kU13cPVp07wjyxfH TtDwuww1fpi6oTi0Eo4NhvM/edit?tab=t.0.

You can see from this example that we chose to list each persona's top needs (such as licenses) on the home page. The teen user would select "Licenses & IDs," where she would find the application requirements and form. The homepage also shows where you can get service—online or in person. So, while the talk bubbles helped us surface the most necessary information, we didn't strictly follow the order of the conversation.

That's a good start. Now we can iterate the content by testing it out with real users.

Testing the content

Task-based testing

Steve Krug popularized qualitative, task-based user testing with his books *Don't Make Me Think!* and *Rocket Surgery Made Easy*. More recently, Erica Jorgensen published her book *Strategic Content Design*. These three books explain how anyone—including the visual and content designers on your team—can test content by showing a product interface to a user and asking the user to accomplish an important task, such as making a purchase, while describing what they're thinking.[11] Because this method is great for finding all kinds of ways to improve a product, content issues naturally come to the fore. I highly recommend that content designers conduct and participate in these types of testing sessions.

After you've conducted task-based user testing to make sure the user can perform the most important actions, it's time to zero in on the content and really polish it up for maximum effectiveness. I have two methods I particularly like to use for this: the User Questions Test and the Highlighter Test.

---

[11] Krug has a great demo of this method on YouTube: https://www.youtube.com/watch?v=1UCDUOB_aS8.

Testing on the macro level: the User Questions Test

While task-based user testing ensures that users can do what you want them to do with your product, the user questions test ensures that people can do what they want to do with your product.

It goes like this. For the first part of the conversation with the user, you don't show them anything. Simply ask them, "Given this type of product, what questions would you have as you navigate to it?"

For example, when I was working on the bank website, I asked users, "Imagine you're navigating to a bank website. What questions would you have? What information would you expect to find there?" The users recited their questions, and I wrote them down. They were things like:

- Is the bank FDIC-insured?
- What types of accounts does the bank have?
- Is this the right bank for someone like me?

That last question came up again and again, which surprised me. In our task-based testing, we would be more likely to ask the user to try to open a checking account than to ask them, "Do you want to know if this bank is right for you?" But in the User Questions Test, it became clear that this question was important to users. When we asked for more details, users clarified that they wanted to know whether they had the right amount of money to bank here. Was this just a bank for wealthy people? Or did the bank want customers who were everyday people like them?

Hearing the users' questions helped us to tailor the content to answer them in a way we wouldn't have been equipped to otherwise.

In the second part of the test, you show the user your product and ask them whether they can find the answers to their questions. Be sure to note whether the user was able to answer each question. Perhaps most importantly, pay special attention to those questions that the user thinks they've found the answer to, but really haven't. If the user asked, "Does the bank offer a high-yield savings account?", and then can't find one, they may conclude that they've found the answer to their question, and it's "No."

If the bank actually does have that savings account, this is an obvious red flag! You've just received an important finding: users can't find a specific content element that's important to them—in this case, information about the savings account—and it's causing them to wrongly conclude that the product they're looking for doesn't exist. If that problem goes into production, it'll really hurt the user experience, and the bank's business.

Testing on the micro level: the Highlighter Test

Sometimes you really want to get into a user's head and understand whether your content is clear on the word level. Do the instructions make sense? Can people understand what the product does? A Highlighter Test works great for this. I've conducted this test in person, but it could also be done remotely using a shared PDF file.

First, you'll want to identify a specific page or set of pages to test. Depending on how long the pages are, you can probably test three or four in an hour-long session.

If you're doing research in person, print out the pages you want to test. Give the first page to the test participant, along with a green highlighter and a pink highlighter. Ask them to read through the pages and highlight content that's helpful in green, and content that's confusing in pink. You can, of course, add more colors and ask the participant to highlight content based on all kinds of impressions. For instance, on an ecommerce site, you could ask them to highlight content that makes them want to buy or not want to buy.

You can follow the same process digitally. Share a PDF of the pages and make sure your participant has an app that allows text highlighting, like Adobe Acrobat Reader.

Then, let the user read and highlight on their own. They can think out loud if they want, but if not, that's fine. After they're done, ask them to walk you through their highlights. Ask them, why is this passage green? Why is that sentence pink? If I'm testing in person, I like to make notes right on the printout to refer to later. If you're testing remotely, you won't be able to easily make notes on the page, but you can type them in a separate document. At the end, you'll have something like Figure 2-10: a printout of a site from the Virginia DMV website that I asked a user to highlight.

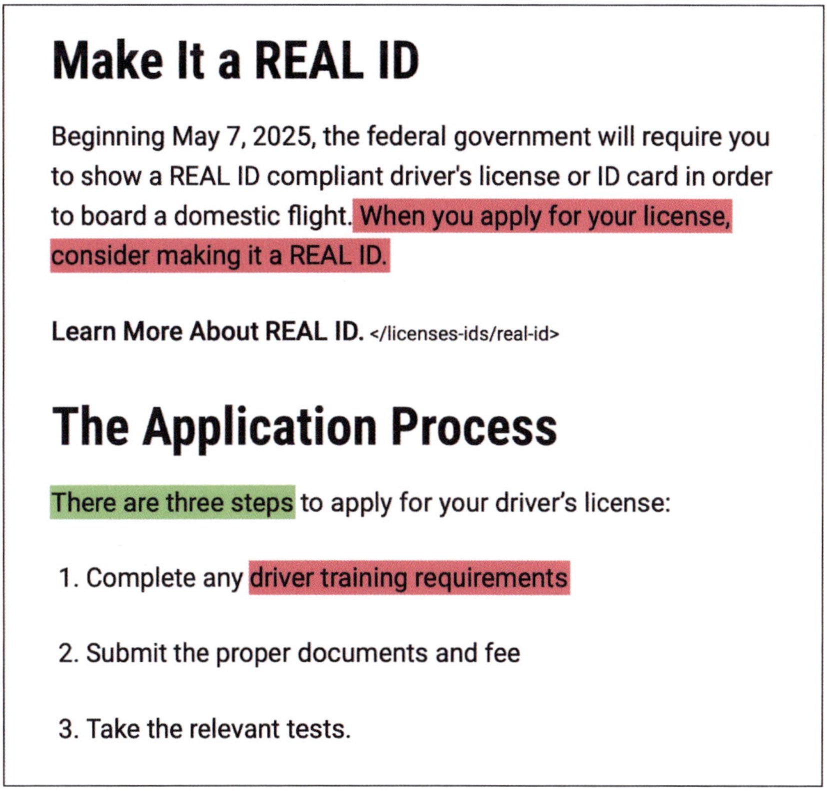

Make It a REAL ID

Beginning May 7, 2025, the federal government will require you to show a REAL ID compliant driver's license or ID card in order to board a domestic flight. When you apply for your license, consider making it a REAL ID.

Learn More About REAL ID. </licenses-ids/real-id>

The Application Process

There are three steps to apply for your driver's license:

1. Complete any driver training requirements

2. Submit the proper documents and fee

3. Take the relevant tests.

Figure 2-10. Highlighting content on the Virginia DMV website.[12]

It's easy to see how the Highlighter Test helps you zero in on micro-sized content successes and failures, and figure out ways of fixing the latter.

---

[12] "Apply for a Driver's License." Virginia DMV. https://www.dmv.virginia.gov/licenses-ids/license/applying.

Bonus: Getting strategic input from content designers

Now that you have a basic understanding of how content designers contribute to the product design process, I want to let you in on a secret: content designers are powerful partners for product strategy and planning, as well.

If part of your job is pitching ideas and features to managers and stakeholders, you may have written two documents developed by Amazon: the six-pager and the PR/FAQ.[13] If you're not familiar with them, here's a quick overview:

- The six-pager is a document that explains an idea in narrative form, taking up six pages at most. Jeff Bezos mandated the use of the six-pager after he decided that "PowerPoint-style presentations somehow give permission to gloss over ideas, flatten out any sense of relative importance, and ignore the interconnectedness of ideas."[14]
- The PR/FAQ is a hypothetical press release with a frequently asked questions appendix that describes a proposed product.[15]

Even though these documents aren't technically part of product design, and are more often classified as part of the product manager's role, content designers can be very helpful in creating them. While you should also be collaborating with your visual design and engineering partners on these documents, content designers in particular help by providing:

---

[13] Bryar, Colin and Carr, Bill. *Working Backwards: Insights, Stories, and Secrets from Inside Amazon.*
[14] Stone, Madeline. July 28, 2015. "A 2004 email from Jeff Bezos explains why PowerPoint presentations aren't allowed at Amazon." *Business Insider.* https://www.businessinsider.com/jeff-bezos-email-against- powerpoint-presentations-2015-7.
[15] Bryar and Carr, 105.

1. *Strategic input.* Chances are good that your content designer has become a subject matter expert in your product area. They may have well informed ideas about the strategic direction of the product that you should consider when writing these documents for your stakeholders.
2. *Tactical writing input.* Of course, content designers are experts in the written word. You need a master storyteller to help you craft your documents with precision and clarity. A content designer is the ideal partner for this.

Deploying content design for your product

Now you know what a content designer does. If you try to do it all, you'll realize that it's a lot of work, especially if you have to also gather content approvals from legal, compliance, or other stakeholders. If you also occupy another role at your company, like UX designer or product manager, you might be thinking, "How am I supposed to do all this?" You're not.[16] That's the point.

Remember what we said in Chapter 1: cognitive diversity is your secret weapon for solving complex problems. One person, or even a team of many people using the same problem-solving methods, by definition lacks cognitive diversity. You need a multidisciplinary team that includes content designers.

The best way to activate content design in your product development process is to hire a content design team the right size for the amount of work you need done. This may sound like common sense, and it is. Yet companies don't do this. Content is invisible to most tech leaders, who estimate work without realizing that products are made out of content.

---

[16] Unless, that is, you work at a tiny startup as the "product team of one," wearing the hats of the PM, designer, researcher, and writer. If you're doing all these things, *my* hat is off to *you*.

I don't know of any companies who actually staff their content design functions properly. They may exist, but I don't know about them.

Be a part of the solution, not the problem. Staff an appropriately sized content design team.

How do you know how many people you need? If you already have a UX design team, you can use the number of designers as a guide. Ideally, you'd have a content designer for each visual UX designer—a 1:1 ratio. If you can't staff content design to that level, at least make sure you don't let the ratio fall below 1:3.

If you don't have a UX design team yet, talk to a visual UX designer, a content designer, and a UX researcher about the work you need done, and get them to estimate how many UX people you need to hire.[17]

So, where do you find this amazing content design team who will write your product for you? Hiring for the right skills is critical, and we'll discuss that in the next chapter.

---

[17] Do not under any circumstances estimate work that you haven't done yourself. Stephen P. Anderson calls this "fact-free planning" in his list of "Bad Problems" (https://docs.google.com/document/d/1JNZBlfKg3FXJQwzDAA7TtkP024MVM97oZnfG_MfmPYw/edit). People who have never done the work underestimate the amount of time and effort it takes. This is true for all disciplines.

CHAPTER 3

HIRING CONTENT DESIGNERS

"Hiring success shouldn't be measured on the start date; instead it should be measured on the first-year anniversary date."

—**LOU ADLER**[1]

In 1908, the following story was published:

> A MORAL WITH AN ENDING.
>
> He was the best machinist in the district, and it was for that reason that the manager had overlooked his private delinquencies. But at last even his patience was exhausted, and [the machinist] was told to go, and another man reigned in his stead at the end of the room.
>
> And then the machine, as though in protest, refused to budge an inch, and all the factory hands were idle. Everyone who knew the difference between a machine and a turnip tried his hand at the inert mass of iron. But

---

[1] Adler, Lou. 2022. *Hire with Your Head* 4th edition, xix.

the machine, metaphorically speaking, laughed at them, and the manager sent for the discharged employee…

He looked at the machine for some moments, and talked to it as a man talks to a horse, and then climbed into its vitals and called for a hammer. There was the sound of a "tap-tap-tap," and in a moment the wheels were spinning, and the man was returning to the "Bull" parlour.

And in the course of time the mill-owner had a bill:–"To mending machine, £10. 10s." And the owner of the works, being as owners go, a poor man, sent a polite note to the man, in which he asked him if he thought tapping a machine with a hammer worth ten guineas. And then he had another bill:—"To tapping machine with hammer, 10s.; to knowing where to tap it, £10; total, £10. 10s."

And the man was reinstated in his position, and was so grateful that he turned teetotaller and lived a great and virtuous old age. And the moral is that a little knowledge is worth a deal of labour.[2]

On digital teams, lots of professionals try their hands at content design. Product managers, designers, researchers, and engineers all find themselves placing words on a screen. And like the machine in the story, the digital product laughs at them:

- People can't use it.
- People abandon it.
- The company's reputation takes a hit.

---

[2] "A Moral with an Ending." *The Journal of the Society of Estate Clerks of Works* 21 (1908): 30. https://www.google.com/books/edition/ The_Journal_of_the_Society_of_Estate_Cle/w-nVAAAAIAAJ.

In that moment, the team realizes that it takes a specialist to know where to tap the content design hammer and get the product usability wheels spinning again. In content design, as in machining, a small effort combined with great knowledge creates immense value.

If you're in this situation, you need to hire a content designer. But make sure that your team is ready, because finding the right content designer for your team requires diligence, on your part and on the team's part. You must implement a process that's free from bias. And when you find the right candidate, you need to make them a compelling offer that includes not just monetary compensation, but time to focus, interesting problems to solve, and a future career path.

BEFORE YOU HIRE A CONTENT DESIGNER

Recognizing that your team needs a skilled content designer is the first step to setting up your new hire for success. But not every team that asks for a content designer is ready for one. Although they may recognize the need, many product managers and designers don't understand how content designers work. They think of a content designer as a service provider: someone who comes in after design has happened, spends a few hours polishing copy, and then floats on to the next project.

Although some content designers may work this way, few content designers want to. On top of the skills required to do the job, it takes a lot of time to understand user and business needs well enough to design product content that meets those needs. It takes even more time to get that content approved by all the necessary stakeholders, then review the final build to make sure it matches the original content design.

Because the content designer should be a full partner in the design process, hiring a content designer should shift ownership of the user experience from one design person (Figure 3-1) to the design team (Figure 3-2). That design team should include the designer, the content designer, and the researcher. Depending on the product, other roles may co-own the experience as well.

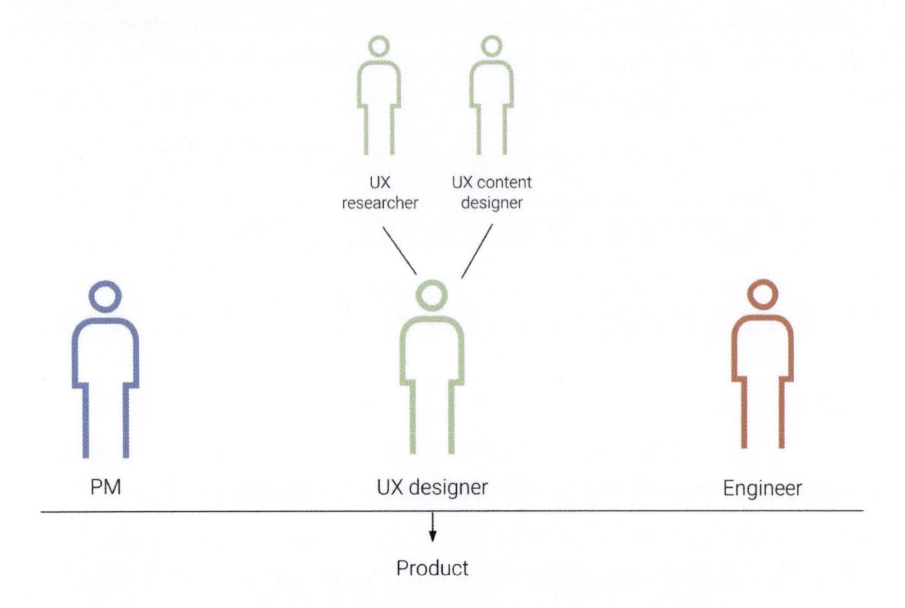

Figure 3-1. In the traditional approach, the visual (UX) designer owns the design. If content and research are assigned, they take on a consulting role.

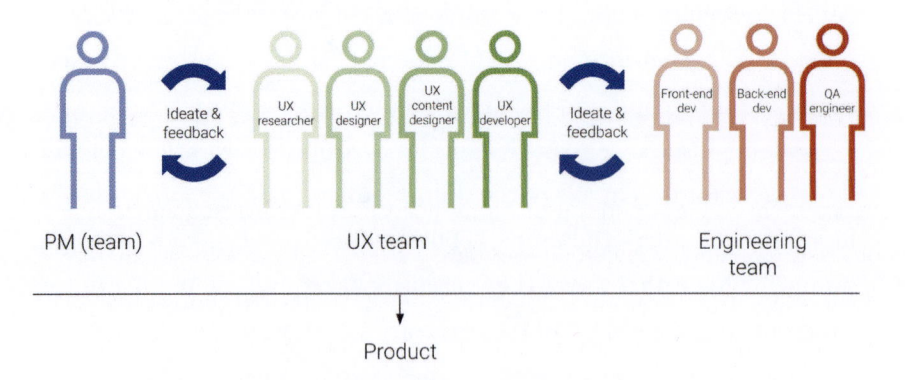

Figure 3-2. In the more effective multidisciplinary approach, a team of UX practitioners takes collective ownership of the design.

This shift in ownership is a big change, because many visual UX designers learned early on—from the hiring habits of startups that I discussed in Chapter 1—that they are the owners of the entire experience, and they've always worked that way.

As a manager, I've hired several content designers. At first, I assumed that just putting content designers onto a team would position them for success. After all, these people were all very smart. They would figure it out!

A few months in, I noticed that one of my new hires was struggling. After talking to her, I realized that it wasn't her fault she was struggling—it was mine. Despite my efforts during the hiring process to clarify her job duties and desired process, I hadn't been clear enough with her team. They didn't know what to do with her, so they didn't include her in important design meetings and decisions. She and I had to have lots of time-consuming and tense discussions with the team about the proper way to work with a content designer.

I learned my lesson. The following year, prior to assigning a new content designer to a team, I discussed his role with the designer. "How do you like to work with a content designer?" I asked.

She responded that she preferred to own the design file, only showing it to the content designer after she finished designing—and sometimes after the design had been shipped into production. Here was a process that would demoralize even the most sanguine of content professionals! I declined to add the content designer to that team, instead assigning him to another team that worked more collaboratively.[3]

Get the design leader on board

I ran into the situation above because I didn't get clear direction—and support—from our design leaders. The broader UX team didn't have a common understanding about the process our leaders expected us to

---

[3] The story has a happy ending: the designer proactively changed her stance and decided to implement a collaborative design process. I assigned the content designer to work with her, and they developed a productive partnership.

follow. If I'd been more insistent in asking our leaders for that direction, it could've saved us the time we spent negotiating how to collaborate.

If you lead design at your organization, I hope that by this point, you're clear on the value of content design. I also hope that you're willing to make your team's UX design process more content-first, as I described in Chapter 2. But if leading design is the job of someone else (usually with the title of director, VP, or Chief Design Officer), you'll need to get that person on board with changing your design process to incorporate content design properly. This will help you avoid confusion and tension later on, because it'll ensure that all the designers, researchers, and content designers understand how they should work together. Talk to your leader about the need for content design on the team. Make sure they know that it's critical to your product's success—and it means completely changing how your designers work. Instead of flying solo, designers will be constantly collaborating in a dynamic trio of visual UX design, content, and research!

Once you get the design leader's agreement, they'll have your back if individual designers resist the new process. You and the design leader will both need to to help the designers understand that the organization is pivoting to a content-first design process because it results in better product experiences for users.

Get the visual UX designer on board

When you hire a content designer, you should explain to the UX designer on the team that they'll be moving to a new content-first design process. On a day-to-day level, the new process will require them to do a few things differently, like:

- Share Edit access to the Figma file
- Add the content designer to their one-on-one meetings with the product manager

- Include the content designer in design critiques, and give them the opportunity to present their work there
- Share design concepts with the content designer before sharing them with the product manager (or other partner outside the design team)
- Refer to the design as "the team's" rather than "mine," and share credit with the content designer and researcher
- Attend a daily design standup to share what they're working on and hear what the content designer is working on
- Treat the content designer's work as a considered design solution, just like the visual designer's own solutions, rather than as "input" or a "recommendation"

Each of these steps is important to setting up the content designer to do their best work. Most visual UX designers will have no problem with them. If your designer hesitates, hear them out and let them know that they'll be a vital part of the hiring and onboarding processes (as you'll see below). They have the opportunity to help you define the scope of the content designer's work. But the points above are non-negotiable if you're going to add a content designer to the team.

Avoid biases when hiring a content designer

Biases are the brain's way of boosting efficiency when it has to process a trillion pieces of information a day. Author David Dylan Thomas defines bias as "a series of shortcuts our minds take that often help but sometimes hurt."[4] Because you're human, avoiding bias when you're hiring requires focus and intention. That's just as true when you hire a content designer as it is when you hire any other role.

---

[4] Thomas, David Dylan. 2020. "Design for Cognitive Bias: Using Mental Shortcuts for Good instead of Evil." https://www.youtube.com/watch?v=7MVRQNJAm-M&t=146s.

The content designer candidate's educational background or resume may not tell you whether they can do the job. As of this writing, in the United States, there is no formal degree program for content design.[5] In fact, the terms UX writing and content design are rarely heard in institutions of higher learning. As a result, the content people you hire may come from a variety of working and educational backgrounds, including journalism, military, public relations, construction, software engineering, psychology, UX design, and more. Unfortunately, there's no shortcut to hiring good content designers. You'll have to put in a lot of work to avoid bias and objectively assess the candidate's skills and experience to determine whether they can do the work you need done.

You want to avoid bias in hiring, but bias has ways of creeping into your hiring process despite your intentions. Here are some do's and don't's based on biases I've seen (or had myself) when hiring content designers.

Don't use snap judgments to rule people out

When I first started hiring many years ago, my attitude was that I would consider candidates until they gave me a reason to rule them out. Unfortunately, that approach put me in a negative mindset while interviewing, because I was always looking for reasons not to hire the person. If they did or said anything unexpected, I was tempted to ask myself, "Is this the sign that they're not right for the job?" A typo in the resume, an unorthodox design solution in the portfolio, or being a few minutes late for an interview had me reconsidering their candidacy.

---

[5] FH Johanneum in Austria has a well regarded master's program in content strategy though: https://www.fh-joanneum.at/content-strategie-und-digitale-kommunikation/master/en/.

But something interesting happened. I somehow hired a candidate who had sent me a very unusual cover letter with a super-quirky tone—and that person was great.

Now I take a positive approach. I look for the candidate's applicable skills and experience using a method called performance-based hiring (we'll dive into this later in the chapter). This approach has allowed me to hire some brilliant content designers.

I once talked to a hiring manager who declared that he wouldn't hire a candidate who wore a suit to the interview, because that candidate clearly wouldn't "fit in" to the casual culture of the company. How unreasonable. How many qualified candidates did he pass up because they couldn't read his mind about the dress code?

It's easier to make a snap judgment and use it to generalize about the candidate's future performance than to carefully assess skills and experience. But it's a huge hiring mistake. Imagine being that poor candidate who was told by a career coach to dress up for an interview, only to get knocked out of consideration due to a hiring manager's shallow prejudice against suit-wearers!

In the UX arena, the most common way I see this play out relates to the visual features of a candidate's portfolio. For content designers especially, this makes no sense. Presentations, including portfolios, could be tweaked a thousand ways. The look and feel, the exact word choice, and the order in which the narrative case studies unfold are all subjective. Yet hiring managers will knock promising candidates out of consideration simply because the manager didn't like a surface-level aspect of the presentation.

It may be controversial, but I don't even rule candidates out of consideration for small typos anymore. That's because I've observed that one or two typos doesn't necessarily mean a candidate isn't a good content designer. What some teammates lack in textual precision, they may make up for in creativity, collaboration skills, narrative chops, or technical knowledge.

We need to diligently avoid making snap judgments. As Lou Adler, author of the book *Hire with Your Head*, says: "It's imperative to prevent biases from creeping into the interview as much as possible in order to make accurate and objective hiring decisions."[6]

DO ASSESS WHAT THEY'VE DONE

When reviewing candidates, you aren't looking for a certain kind of person. Don't label people based on what you think they are ("she's more of a marketer," "he's not really leader material") or have ("she has a Master's degree," "he has experience at Meta"). Thinking in these ways is a recipe for unleashing your unconscious biases.

For example, advanced degrees are great—I have one—but they're not necessary to do the work. Neither is a certain personality type: the candidate could be extroverted or introverted, cheerful or taciturn, charismatic or awkward, and still be good at their job. I've known effective content designers who meet each of these descriptions.

Looking at the candidate's past actions—their specific skills and experience—is far more helpful than looking at their attributes. Adler notes, "If it can be proven during the interview that a candidate has successfully handled similar work, it's clear the person has all of the skills and experiences necessary."[7] And "similar work" doesn't mean the exact same task. Can the candidate with a journalism background show how she carefully researched her sources while writing an article? Those research skills are directly transferable to content design, if the candidate is motivated to make the transition.

Of course, you must know exactly what you need your new content designer to accomplish before you can assess whether a candidate has evidence of relevant skills and experiences. That's why the

---

[6] Adler, 41.
[7] ibid.

performance-based hiring process starts with a thorough investigation of your open role, as we'll see later.

DO ASSESS "CULTURE ADD" INSTEAD OF CULTURE FIT

In June of 2017, Uber fired over 20 employees after a whistleblower alleged that she had been subjected to sexual harassment and, after she reported the harassment, retaliation.[8] CEO Travis Kalanick was forced to resign due to the toxic work culture he had allowed. The following year, the company settled a $10 million class action lawsuit for discrimination, harassment, and a hostile work environment.[9]

How do the cultures at some tech companies become bro-tastic bubbles of toxicity? Teams just keep hiring people who look like them, think like them, and don't question their unhealthy cultural norms. It's only natural to identify with someone who reminds you of yourself or shares characteristics with you. Bonding over a shared alma mater, hometown, or taste in indie bands makes it easy to feel an instant connection. This tendency is called affinity bias. For too many managers, the hiring process is simply a drawn-out process of assessing affinity—similarity to the manager individually, or to the team as a group.

Don't fall into the trap of looking for "culture fit." It's just plain dumb to hire someone only because you like them. Liking someone doesn't mean they'll be good at the job, and not feeling an instant rapport doesn't mean they'll be bad at the job.

Instead, be open to someone different. Are they quiet while the rest of the team is boisterous? That's fine. Do they work slowly and

---

[8] Solon, Olivia. June 6, 2017. "Uber fires more than 20 employees after sexual harassment investigation." *The Guardian.* https://www.theguardian.com/technology/2017/jun/06/uber-fires-employees-sexual-harassment-investigation.

[9] Outten & Golden. "Uber equal pay and harassment class action." https://www.outtengolden.com/capabilities/cases/uber-equal-pay-and-harassment-class-action/.

deliberately while you rush to solutions? Great. Do they go home after work while the rest of the team hangs out and plays cornhole? Their life experience might bring a much-needed new perspective to the work. Don't write them off because they're not like you.

As *Forbes* says, "If you want your business to stretch into new markets, areas or industries, it's going to take new and novel perspectives to get there. Instead of hiring for culture fit, hire for culture add to inject new energy and ideas into your business."[10]

3 STEPS TO PERFORMANCE-BASED HIRING

To hire the right content designer, you need to understand what your organization needs them to do. You'll then use this information to create a performance-focused job description (also called a performance profile). This allows you to hire a candidate who will be as successful on their one-year anniversary as they were in the interview, increasing the likelihood that you, the new employee, and the team are all happy with the hire.[11]

Step 1: Run a hiring workshop

You may be the hiring manager, but in order to hire the right content designer, you need input from the team who'll spend most of their time working with them. What does the team expect their future content design co-worker to do? A lightweight hiring workshop can answer this question. Jared Spool says, "The idea is simple: get the team together and

---

[10] Montgomery, Louis, Jr. Jun 8, 2022. "Culture Fit vs. Culture Add: Hiring for Growth." *Forbes.* https://www.forbes.com/councils/forbeshumanresourcescouncil/2022/06/08/culture-fit-versus-culture-add-hiring-for-growth/.
[11] Adler, 14.

describe what the work will be like for their new team member."[12] The workshop doesn't need to be time-consuming. In less than an hour, you can glean insights from the team that can set you up to avoid interview chaos and hire a winning candidate.

First, get the team together. In an established company, we're probably talking about a product manager, a researcher, and a visual designer or two. Maybe even an engineer or marketer. Each of these people has expectations about what the content designer will do, and it's your job to find out what these expectations are. If you're in person, grab a whiteboard and stickies. If you're virtual, fire up Figjam, Miro, Mural, or your favorite whiteboarding app.

If your workplace is anything like mine, getting time on people's calendars is almost as hard as expensing a first-class plane ticket. So I've taken an established workshop and shortened it to 35 minutes, to get the most input out of the team in a small amount of time (see Figure 3-3).[13]

---

[12] Jared Spool, "UX Hiring: The Performance Profile is a Game Changer." *Center Centre*. https://articles.centercentre.com/ux-hiring-the-performance-profile-is-a-game-changer/.

[13] This workshop is an abbreviated and adapted version of one described by Avore, Chris and Unger, Russ, *Liftoff! Practical Design Leadership to Elevate Your Team, Your Organization, and You*, 64.

Timing	Task	Who does it
5 minutes	**Introduction** Explain that you'll be coming up with requirements for the content design role.	Hiring manager
5 minutes	**Share ideas** Answer on stickies: What will this content designer do in their first year?	Full team
15 minutes	**Group ideas** Each person reads what they wrote down. Group similar tasks and label each group.	Full team
5 minutes	**Vote** Using sticky dots or virtual stickers, each person votes on the 3–5 most important tasks.	Full team
5 minutes	**Debrief** Explain that you'll compile the performance profile based on the discussion.	Hiring manager

Figure 3-3. An agenda for a quick hiring workshop.

First, explain the purpose of the meeting: to come to an agreement about what the content designer will be expected to accomplish in their first year. Then, set a timer for 5 minutes. Have each team member write down on a sticky note one task that the content designer should have completed a year from now. Your goal is to get to specifics, like "work with the researcher to identify the questions we need to answer, help write study plans, and participate in user interviews." If the tasks start out sounding more general, like "collaborate with research," you can work toward specificity in the ensuing discussion.

When the five minutes are up, it's time for affinity mapping. Have each person read their tasks out loud to the rest of the group. Group the stickies by topic as people read. Discuss any surprises. Does the product manager expect the content designer to write blog posts? Does the visual designer expect to write the UI copy herself and have the new hire proofread it? Discard any expectations that you, as the hiring manager, are sure that you disagree with, or that the team can't agree on, while explaining that that task isn't in the content designer's scope of work.

This is your first chance to set the working team's expectations of the new content designer. Be diplomatic but clear when you identify expectations that are clearly not appropriate. (Sorry, product manager, but most content designers don't have time to write blog posts on a weekly basis.) Your group will come up with a lot of suitable tasks that everyone can agree on. Work together to identify labels for each group of agreed-upon tasks.

Now it's time to vote. Set the timer for 5 minutes again. When workshopping in person, I like to use "sticky dots" for voting. Most virtual platforms (like Miro and Figjam) offer digital stamps or stickers for this. Give each person on the team 3–5 votes, and let them vote for the tasks that they think are most important. Keep the votes at the task level, rather than the category level. That way, when you go to write the performance profile, you can put the most-voted tasks at the top of the list.

With that, you're done! Explain to the team that you'll use the results of the workshop to write the performance profile, then you'll circulate it amongst the team for their review and approval.

Example: The CapyTravel hiring workshop

Capybara Software Company needs a content designer to work on their flagship product CapyTravel, an app that lets travel agents create custom trips for travelers. The hiring manager, Jan, virtually gathers the team—comprising the product manager, visual UX designer, UX researcher, and a content designer who works on a sister product—to discuss expectations for the new content designer.

After introducing the premise of the workshop, Jan asks, "What will this content designer do in their first year?"

Each person on the team takes 5 minutes to write their ideas on stickies in Figjam.

Then, they group them by category and dot-vote on their favorites. Jan notices that they came up with 5 categories:

1. Core content design tasks
2. Content standards
3. Product expertise
4. Collaboration
5. Research

After the meeting, Jan consolidates the agreed-upon tasks into a performance profile.

Step 2: Write the performance profile

Now that you have the output of the hiring workshop, it's up to you to draft the job description. You don't want to write just any old boilerplate listing. You want one that compels the right content designer to apply—because they understand what the job entails—while it also sets them up for success.

Enter the performance profile. To quote Lou Adler, "A performance-based job description, also called a performance profile, describes the work a person needs to do to be successful, not the skills and experiences required to do the work."[14]

---

[14] Adler, 79.

Example: Performance Profile for CapyTravel Content Designer (mid-level)

Here's the performance profile that Jan compiled based on the CapyTravel hiring workshop.

Core content design tasks

- Learn about CapyTravel and propose related opportunities
- Write clear, usable content for CapyTravel design projects
- Work with stakeholders in different time zones
- Gather feedback from salespeople and findings from UX research to identify opportunities to improve content on existing surfaces within the CapyTravel app
- Strengthen content cohesion between CapyTravel and sister product CapyRent by partnering with the CapyRent content designer
- Use Figma to iterate on designs, provide comments, and update prototypes

Standards

- Understand the Traveler and Agent user personas and create voice and tone standards for communicating with each
- Create and maintain content guidelines for the CapyTravel app with input the cross-functional team

Product expertise

- Participate in object mapping to define core concepts for CapyTravel, and share those core concepts with the team
- Gain subject matter expertise in CapyTravel and represent the product to the rest of the content design team when they have questions or need partnership

Collaboration

- Share ideas in working sessions with designers and researchers
- Participate in quarterly planning by proposing ideas and estimating sizes for content tasks
- Deliver content according to agreed timelines, clearly communicating with the product manager when deliveries are at risk
- Participate in weekly meetings to inform product managers about work in progress, UX research findings, and UX proposals

Research

- Attend research sessions, help synthesize findings, participate in readouts, and implement recommendations
- Propose and perform research that informs content solutions
- Attend research briefings for our other products to understand broader user needs and experiences and how CapyTravel fits into the Capybara product ecosystem
- Continually learn about content-based research methods

Step 3: Interview content designers

Now that you know what you expect of your new hire, you can design your hiring process. Creating a good hiring process is a balancing act: make it too long, and qualified candidates will drop out. Make it too short, and the hiring panelists will simply assess the candidate's likeability—the precursor to a biased hiring decision.

The sample performance profile above has 18 bullets. Each interviewer should be assigned 3-4 of those bullets, in order to assess whether the candidate has accomplished something similar before. The interview sequence varies from one organization to another, but a typical sequence looks something like this.

Recruiter screening (15 to 30 minutes)

This is where the recruiter gives the candidate a rundown of the job requirements: is it remote or onsite? Who will the candidate work with? What will they work on? The candidate can ask basic questions about the organization and role. The recruiter may also ask a few basic questions about the candidate's experience.

Hiring manager interview (30 minutes to 1 hour)

In this interview, the candidate meets the hiring manager for the first time. If you're the hiring manager, you'll have a set of expectations from the performance profile, and you'll be asking the candidate to "tell me about a time when" they did something similar to each. Prepared candidates should be able to recount their relevant experience using the STAR format: Situation, Task, Action, Result.[15]

Portfolio review with hiring panel (1 hour, 3–5 participants)

The portfolio review is the candidate's chance to walk the hiring panel through one or two specific projects and show how the candidate contributed to the projects' success. After the presentation, each panelist will have a chance to ask questions to better assess whether the candidate's experience fits the performance profile.

If you're a panelist, avoid asking questions that don't help you assess the candidate's experience, just because you're curious or interested in the subject matter. If the candidate worked on a cool app, that's great! But even if you're burning to ask how the app grew its user base to 1 million in a year, if it isn't relevant to the performance profile you're hiring for,

---

[15] "The STAR Method." GOV.UK National Careers Service. https://nationalcareers.service.gov.uk/careers-advice/interview-advice/the-star-method.

resist the temptation to ask. You can always connect on LinkedIn and talk app growth later!

One-on-one interviews with team members (30 minutes each; usually there are 2 to 4 of these)

These interviews give the candidate a chance to meet other future co-workers who may not have joined the hiring panel. They can also allow interviewers who did see the portfolio presentation to ask more specific questions about the candidate's experience.

Designing efficient interviews

4–5 hours of interviews is a lot of time, both for the hiring panel and the candidate. But the hiring panel needs to spend that much time to assess the candidate's skills and experience.

In order to determine who's on your interview panel, ask yourself, who were the people in the hiring workshop? They're probably the ones who should be assessing the candidate in interviews.

If you've been on the job market before, you know a typical slate of interview questions is all over the place. I've had skilled and focused interviewers, but I've also seen interviewers wing it, ask the same questions as their teammates, banter idly, and even come up blank when it's their turn to ask a question. As the hiring manager, you can avoid that kind of chaos by assigning each interviewer a performance area to assess.

Interview like a scientist

Notice I said "assess." This isn't a vibe check—you have to be objective in order to avoid bias. Let's think like scientists: we want to determine whether the candidate has provided sufficient evidence that they can do each required task listed in the performance profile. They can provide this evidence either by credibly telling you about a time they actually performed the task or, if they've never done the task before, by demonstrating transferable skills plus motivation.

For example, one of the tasks required of the new CapyTravel content designer is to "Learn about CapyTravel and propose related opportunities." The interviewer assigned to assess this performance area might ask the following question: "Tell me about a time you had to learn about a new product. What actions did you take? What happened as a result?" In response, the candidate might say something like this:

> When I worked at BestCo, my role was to edit our blog for car enthusiasts—but I didn't know a thing about automobiles. So I asked if I could listen in on as many research sessions as possible to learn about our customers. I also listened in on support calls and talked to salespeople. I learned all about our audience, the terms they used, and the problems they had. In my first six months I was able to propose a dozen article ideas, three of which ended up sending a total of 5 million qualified visitors to our ecommerce site.

In this example, even though the candidate didn't work on an app, she demonstrated comparable experience learning a technical domain and finding new opportunities, then delivering on them. If she's motivated to work on an app (something the interviewer can suss out during the rest of the conversation), she'll likely do a great job on CapyTravel.

Communicate with the candidate

Your recruiter may be the one who describes the interview process to the candidate. If so, great! But as the hiring manager, you should double-check that the candidate understands the process. There are few things worse than clearing five people's calendars for an hourlong portfolio review, only for the candidate to join and tell you that they had no idea they were expected to present. Confirm with the candidate beforehand.

In addition to explaining the process, check in before each interview and let the candidate know what you'll be asking. That's right—you should give the candidate your interview questions before the interview if at all possible. Unless you work in an organization where they'll need to come up with solutions on the fly (spoiler: most of us don't), there's no need to cause unnecessary stress by springing questions on the candidate. Giving candidates a chance to think about the question and their answer results in deeper discussions, better evidence, and better hiring decisions.

Design interview guides for your panel

If you're the hiring manager, don't leave your interview panel to "wing it." Make them interview guides. The interview guide is based on the performance profile, and it ensures that each interviewer assesses the candidate's ability to perform a relevant task—in other words, it helps them do the opposite of wing it. Most interviewers appreciate knowing what to look for and will thank you for your guidance!

Assign each interviewer a set of tasks from the performance profile. The interviewer's job is to determine, based on evidence provided by the candidate, whether the candidate has done something comparable or transferable, and whether they have sufficient motivation to do the work. You'll also be assigning sample questions for each task the interviewer is assessing. Asking for evidence of comparable experience ("Tell me about a time…") feels a bit formal, but enables the interviewers to dig deep enough to understand whether the candidate actually did the work they claimed they did. It also keeps the conversation focused on comparable experience, rather than allowing the interviewer to make the conversation a friendly chat where they judge the candidate based on their personality or likeability.

Each interviewer should score the candidate's responses from 1 to 5. Numerically scoring each performance factor prevents each interviewer from collapsing their opinion into a single "yes/no" judgment, which can be a Trojan horse for bias. It's too easy to decide you like someone in the first 5 minutes and issue a "yes," only to find out later that they're unqualified. Similarly, you may decide you dislike someone and issue a "no" without fairly weighing the merits of their skills and experience. Adler describes the scores this way:[16]

- Level 1: Minimal skill set (unqualified)
- Level 2: Adequate skill set (marginally qualified)
- Level 3: Strong performer (top third of candidates)
- Level 4: Great performer (top 20% of candidates)
- Level 5: Outstanding performer (top 10% of candidates)

A successful candidate will score all 3s or above.

Example: Interview Guide for CapyTravel Content Designer (mid-level)

The interview guide (see Figure 3-4) contains the tasks from the performance profile (see the column titled "Performance item to assess"), but not necessarily in the same order. That's because the performance profile grouped tasks by similarity, while the interview guide groups tasks by which person can best assess them.

---

[16] Adler, 160.

Panel member (role)	Performance items this person will assess	Questions	Score (1-5)
Jan (hiring manager)	• Understand the Traveler and Agent personas and create voice and tone standards for each • Create and maintain content guidelines for CapyTravel overall with input the cross-functional team • Learn the CapyTravel problem space and propose opportunities relating to CapyTravel • Work with stakeholders in different time zones	• Tell me about a time when you worked with personas. How did you use them in your work? • Have you created and maintained content guidelines for a product? If so, tell me about it. • Tell me about a time when you needed to quickly learn about a new problem space. • Have you ever worked with stakeholders in different time zones?	
Joey (peer content designer)	• Write clear, usable content for design projects • Gather feedback from Sales and findings from UX Research to identify opportunities to improve content on existing surfaces within CapyTravel • Strengthen content cohesion between CapyTravel and sister product CapyRent by partnering with the CapyRent content designer • Understand or learn to use Figma to iterate on designs, provide comments, and update prototypes	• *(Interviewer should review the candidate's portfolio for writing quality.)* • Have you ever gathered findings from Sales or Research? How did you turn the data into content improvements? • Tell me about a time when you worked with a peer content designer who was assigned to a related product area. What was your process like? • Tell me about a time when you needed to learn a design tool in order to work with a team.	

Ramona (researcher)	• Attend research sessions, help synthesize findings, participate in readouts, and implement recommendations • As needed, propose and perform research that informs content solutions • Attend research readouts for other products to understand broader user needs and experiences and how CapyTravel fits into the Capybara product ecosystem • Continually learn about content-based research methods	• Have you participated in usability research before? What did that look like? • Tell me about a time when you proposed a research project. • How have you incorporated research findings into your process? • Do you have any favorite research methods? How do you learn about new methods?	
Ian (designer)	• Participate in object mapping to define and socialize core concepts for CapyTravel • Gain subject matter expertise in CapyTravel and represent the product to the rest of the content design team when they have questions or need partnership • Ideate in working sessions with designers and researchers	• Have you participated in concept mapping with the team? • Tell me about a time when you needed to become a subject matter expert in a product. How did you work with other product teams to ensure cohesion in the product ecosystem? • Have you worked on a team with designers and researchers? How did you work together?	
Elizabeth (product manager)	• Participate in quarterly planning by proposing ideas and estimating sizes for content tasks • Deliver content according to agreed timelines, clearly communicating with the	• Tell me about a time when you had to plan or estimate your work. • Have you ever missed a deadline? How did you communicate the updated timeline to your	

| | Product Manager when deliveries are at risk
• Participate in weekly meetings to inform PMs about work in progress, UX Research findings, and UX proposals | stakeholders and teammates?
• Have you worked with a product manager before? How did you keep them up-to-date on research findings and your ideas for improving the product? | |

Figure 3-4. The interview guide for the CapyTravel Content Designer role.

Explain to your interviewers that they should use the interview guide and seek to assess evidence of comparable experience, rather than making snap judgments based on personality or other subjective factors. Let them know that you expect them to take notes that include the evidence they found and the rating for each of their assigned factors. That should prepare them to discuss their findings in the debrief.

Debriefing the interview

By this point, your interview panel should already know that they're not being asked to issue a *Gladiator*-style thumbs up or thumbs down on the candidate—a proceeding which is far too subjective and prone to bias. If they've listened to your instructions, the interviewers wrote notes summarizing the evidence they found, along with their scores.

When debriefing the portfolio review, ask interviewers to read their evidence to the group. The entire group should then come to an agreement about whether the candidate will proceed. Try to avoid allowing one person to sway the group based on subjective judgments like, "She didn't seem very likable," or "He was just awkward." If an interviewer does show signs of bias, discuss it with the recruiter after the meeting. Either you or the recruiter should follow up with that interviewer and explain that your standards for interviewing don't allow for bias.

Once you find a candidate who gets all 3s and above for the factors your team interviewed for, work with your recruiter to make a compelling offer. That offer should include not just monetary compensation, but interesting work with a collaborative team, a chance to give input to the product strategy, and a promising career path.

Once you've made the offer and the candidate has accepted it, you should take a deep breath and appreciate what you've accomplished. You've hired your first content designer by identifying the content work that you need them to do, then matching their skills and experience to the job. It was a lot of work, but now you have a great process you can revisit every time you need to hire.

Next, you'll need to know how to onboard and manage your content designer. Don't fret—Chapter 4 will explain how.

CHAPTER 4

MANAGING CONTENT DESIGNERS

"Just like how there is no one way to go about being a person, there is no one way to go about managing a group of people."
— JULIE ZHUO

ONBOARDING YOUR NEW HIRE

Have you ever started a job that took forever to get the hang of? One of the worst parts of a new job is knowing you don't understand enough to contribute anything meaningful. It's not a great feeling. Good onboarding can minimize that frustration for your new hire and help them contribute more value, more quickly.

Before your new hire starts, make them a document with the important information they'll need. It could be a Word doc, a PowerPoint presentation, or another type of document. As with most things, the format doesn't matter as much as the content. Here's what you should be sure to include:

- *People*: Who are the important stakeholders the new hire will work with? Who's in their reporting chain? Be sure to include an org chart depicting reporting structures for the content team, the visual design team, the research team, the product team, and if possible, the engineering team as well.
- *Meetings*: Be sure to add your new hire to the meetings they'll need to attend.
    - *One-on-ones*: If you're the manager, be sure to schedule one-on-one meetings for at least 45 minutes per week. You'll want to keep a notes document for this meeting and let the content designer set the agenda. What questions do they have? What do they need from you? Don't take up the one-on-one by asking for a status update—they can give you that asynchronously. This is their time.
    - *Product team meetings*: Most product teams have a standing weekly meeting for the product manager and UX team to sync up. Ask the team to add the content designer to those meetings. The team should also add the content designer to their project-related working sessions and sprint meetings (Chapter 5 will show you what a full sprint schedule that includes content design might look like).
    - *Design reviews*: Some organizations have virtually no design reviews—once the product manager, visual designer, content designer, and engineers are happy with the solution, they ship it. Other orgs have multiple levels of reviewers, from lead designers, to managers, to VPs and directors, possibly even up to the C-suite. Explain to your new hire exactly what rounds of approvals their designs will go through.
- *Tools*: Be sure to ask the admins to provision the various required tools to the content designer. At a minimum, the new hire will need Edit access to Figma, as well as access to whatever ticketing system, whiteboarding tool, and analytics tool your team uses.

- *Deliverables*: Sharing past project deliverables with the content designer will be super helpful in bringing your new hire up to speed fast. They'll be able to see how the designers have delivered content in the past (after all, someone's been doing the content work!). Help them understand what has worked and what hasn't.
- *Projects in flight*: What's the team working on? Provide the new hire with a breakdown of the work the team has shipped in the past few months, what they're doing now, and what's on the product roadmap for the next three to six months.

When you ran the hiring workshop, you had the chance to set the team's expectations about how to work with the content designer. Now you'll want to take every opportunity to remind the working team—the product manager, visual designers, researcher, and engineers—that the content designer will be a full partner in the design process.

And the new content designer? You'll need to manage them through their transition onto the team. Your performance as a manager is the single biggest determiner of their satisfaction with the job. No pressure.

The manager makes or breaks the team

I sat alone in the little conference room and cried. I had just learned that my manager was leaving the company. But I wasn't crying because I was emotionally attached to my manager, I was crying because I knew that I would now have to report to his boss.

This leader had a reputation for being toxic. He was mercurial—friendly one second, angrily defending himself against some perceived slight the next. You never knew whether he was going to congratulate you on a job well done, or fire you. It was exhausting.

Sitting by myself in that conference room, I dried my tears and steeled my resolve. I could do it. I would agree with whatever he said. Surely, that would keep me on his good side!

It didn't. Six disastrous weeks (and three nerve-shredding one-on-one meetings) later, I started looking for a new job. I had loved working at this company, but I couldn't stay. The cost to my sanity was too great.

I've worked for many managers in my career. Some were great, others were terrible. What the good managers had in common was a mindset of servant leadership—the belief in putting their teammates' needs ahead of their own self-interest.[1]

Coaching content designers

Now that you've hired one or more content designers, you have to coach them. I define coaching as helping your direct report perform the job duties well. Fortunately, you know the content designer's job duties because you've already created the performance profile for the role.

Like any other manager, the manager of content designers should think of their role as supporting the team, rather than exercising power over them. After all, the content designer is the one who's actually changing the product, making it better for users every day. As the manager, you should be asking yourself: what can I do to help them? How can I make their job easier? This will require you to do what bad managers don't: to put aside your own insecurities. It's not about you anymore. You have a team relying on you.

Coaching people is a huge topic—one that has filled many a book—and I won't cover it exhaustively here.[2] But I do think that coaching content designers has some qualities that are, if not totally unique, at least distinctive. In my time as a content design manager, I've noticed

---

[1] The practice of servant leadership has been shown by scientific research to improve team performance. See for example Liden, Robert et al, "Servant Leadership and Serving Culture: Influence on Individual and Unit Performance." https://journals.aom.org/doi/abs/10.5465/amj.2013.0034.

[2] For a deep dive into people management and coaching, I recommend Zhuo, Julie, *The Making of a Manager*.

that content designers tend to fall into three categories with regard to their work performance:

- High performing
- Performing
- Underperforming

No one is pinned to one of these categories forever. I've fallen into each of the three categories at different times in my career, depending on what was happening in my life and in the organization at the time. Given the right conditions and coaching, most underperforming content designers can improve. It's on you, the manager, to do everything you can (within reason) to help them reach their potential.

You'll coach each content designer differently. Let's take a closer look at what each performance category means and how you should coach it.

HIGH PERFORMING

What it looks like

This content designer is having a great time at work. They're a super-smart high achiever, and the team recognizes it. They have no problem getting invited to the kickoff meeting, or any meeting, because their teammates know that content's role is central to the design process. The team comes to this content designer with questions—not just about commas and capitalization, but about product strategy. This content designer leads workshops, working sessions, kickoffs, and perhaps even the entire design process. When it's time for their yearly review, they get glowing feedback from teammates, and have no problem coming up with data to show how their content work has affected the business. For example, this content designer can explain how they improved an error message that prevented user churn and increased the company's revenue.

How to manage them

I'll sum up managing a high performer in five words: get out of the way! While their work will need to go through your organization's standard approval process (what that looks like will be unique to your org), you don't need to insert yourself into every discussion or micro-manage every decision. If they design a solution that's different from what you'd come up with, but have data to back it up, let it be. This content designer has earned credibility. While you'll need to provide feedback just as you would to any member of your team, don't be too heavy-handed in giving direction.

Challenges

One challenge of managing a high performer is getting them to tell you when they're burning out. This content designer loves their work and may volunteer to work late hours or weekends. If this happens over time, that's a recipe for degraded mental health and low morale. Don't risk letting one of your highest performers run themselves ragged! Encourage them to take time off and maintain a reasonable balance of working time and personal time.

Be sure not to take this content designer for granted. Familiarize yourself with your organization's promotion process. This content designer knows their value and may begin asking for a deserved raise or promotion. You don't want to lose them because your request for their promotion got caught up in some organizational red tape that you weren't aware of. A great manager once told me, "Talent will find a home." Even when it's hard to find a rewarding job, a talented person will figure out how to make it happen. So, even in an employer's labor market, pay your content designers what they're worth. That includes advocating for their raise or promotion when you have the evidence to make a good case for it to your leaders.

Performing

What it looks like

This content designer is making an impact, yet sometimes runs into roadblocks, like being left out of a meeting or strategic conversation. They may still be learning how to do certain things, such as running workshops or helping with user research. Their team sees them as a valuable contributor, but may limit their questions to content-related ones. When it's time for this content designer's review, they get positive feedback, but the cross-functional team mainly sees them as a writing specialist rather than a design thinker, which may frustrate the content designer at times. This category will represent the majority of your content design team.

How to manage them

There's an art to knowing when to lean in and provide more direction, and when to stand back and let this content designer run with their ideas. You'll definitely need to be on hand to provide feedback, to ensure that they're delivering good content. If you disagree with a solution they come up with, they may not have data or a compelling rationale to back it up. In those cases, you might have to gently recommend a different solution by asking questions like, "Does this solve X problem?" or "What about user Y?" or "Have you considered this other idea?" At other times, especially when the stakes are low, such as when user research will be conducted right away, it'll be worth letting them try out their ideas to see if they get good results.

Challenges

Encourage the Performing content designer to up-level their skills by attending conferences or taking courses. You may even identify someone on the team who's an expert in a certain area, and have that person tutor this content designer.[3] For example, I once managed a content designer who was an expert in Figma. Variables and auto layout were no mystery to him! In our weekly team meetings, he would tutor the team on various technical aspects of Figma, and he even created a dedicated board for the team to put his lessons into practice. The Performing content designers on the team appreciated his mentorship greatly.

Help the Performing content designer to see themselves as a strategic thinker, rather than just an order taker. Taking cues from the cross-functional team, the content designer may assume that their role is limited to just making language "recommendations" for the UI. That's a reductive view of content design, and one that limits the content designer's ability to help their team achieve the cognitive diversity that, as we saw in Chapter 1, will help it to effectively solve complex problems.

Underperforming

What it looks like

Managing an Underperformer is perhaps the greatest challenge you can face as a manager. One reason for this is that content designers who are Underperforming need a disproportionate amount of your time and energy.

It's typical for teams not to know the best way to engage with a content designer. A successful content designer anticipates this and learns how to diplomatically but firmly inform their team how them likes to collaborate (typically, early and often). An unsuccessful content designer, however, does not do this effectively. For whatever reason, the Underperforming content designer has a hard time rolling with the more difficult aspects of the job, like being left out of meetings and decisions.

---

[3] Rachel McConnell offers a good method of assessing your team's collective capabilities in *Leading Content Design*, 37.

Often, this content designer is having a tough time at work and not enjoying their role.

How to manage them

Take extra time with this content designer to listen to their frustrations. Often, just hearing them out is all it takes to help them to feel supported. In some cases, you may be able to do something about the problem, like meeting with the product manager or visual designer to explain that you expect the content designer to be included in the entire design process. Part of your job as a manager is to make sure the cross-functional team understands that content design is a design function, not a service your team provides to visual UX designers. Try to help the team see that, without content, visual design is pointless, and that's why the content designer is such an integral team member.

Challenges

If you followed the performance-based hiring process I described in Chapter 3, you shouldn't have a content designer on your team who struggles to write well. But maybe you didn't hire everyone on your team, but inherited the team from another manager. If you do end up with a content designer who struggles with the craft of writing, you'll need a sharp editing eye (or you'll need to partner with someone who has one). For better or worse, you'll need to catch any mistakes or bad ideas and suggest better ones.

When managing an Underperforming content designer, be very clear with your expectations and give specific, actionable feedback. For example, "you seem frustrated" is not good feedback. Is it really your job as a manager to police your team's feelings? Instead, say something like, "Criticizing the visual designer's work in front of the client is not productive, because it undermines the client's confidence in our team.

Please provide your feedback and solutions to the designer before client meetings instead."

Most organizations have a Human Resources (HR) team that can help guide you through coaching an Underperformer, but it's important to remember that HR's primary job is to protect the company from liability, not to help the content designer improve their performance. By all means, do what HR tells you, but they're not the manager, so they're not as invested in the content designer's success as you are. You'll want to go above and beyond in providing feedback on the content designer's work. Make sure you document all problems you discuss with the content designer, including your expectations and the next steps you asked them to complete. A one-on-one notes document works well for this.

If your attention and feedback don't seem to help, know that people who underperform as content designers are usually talented in other areas. I've known content designers who transitioned into user research or visual design roles. Content design can be hard, and it's not for everyone. Have an honest discussion with the content designer about whether this role is right for them. If their true interests and talents lie elsewhere, you may be able to find a better match for them within your organization.

CHAPTER 5

THE COLLABORATIVE DESIGN SPRINT

"Content precedes design. Design in the absence of content is not design, it's decoration."
—JEFFREY ZELDMAN

Adequately staffing a content design team sets up the larger UX team for a successful working collaboration. However, we know from previous chapters that content design teams are rarely adequately staffed.

Understaffing content designers is so common that, in her book *Leading Content Design*, Rachel McConnell coined a term for it: the content trap, a "vicious cycle that keeps [content] teams stuck doing low-impact work." When visual designers can allocate 100% of their time to a problem that a content designer can only devote 10–20% of their time to, the content designer can't have as much impact on the product, degrading the entire design collaboration. This reinforces the organization's view that content work offers little value. Content designers find this demoralizing, to say the least.

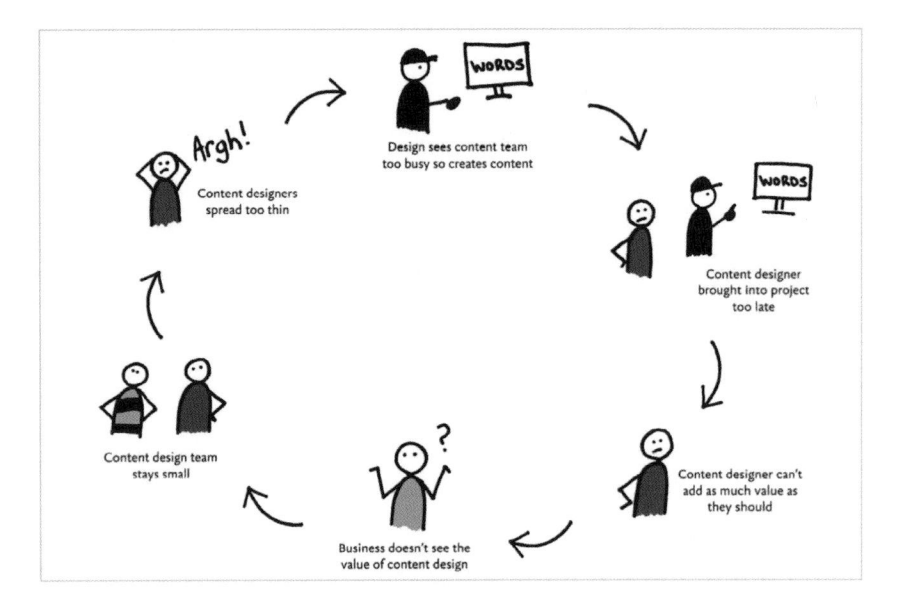

Figure 5-1. Rachel McConnell's "content trap" shows how inadequate content design staffing results in an ineffective design collaboration, which in turn worsens staffing levels even more.[1]

True multidisciplinary UX collaboration requires teams to do a few things differently:

1. *Share accountability.* Above, we listed the problems that arise when we treat content design as a supporting service to visual UX design. The solution is to adequately staff these roles and hold all UX practitioners (including both visual designers and content designers) equally accountable for product outcomes. To do this, content designers must be empowered to practice what writer Beth Dunn calls "full-stack content design."[2] This means working alongside UX designers on deeper levels of the product—like mapping the system objects and the conversation underpinning the design, as we did in Chapter 2.

---

[1] McConnell, Rachel. 2022. *Leading Content Design*, 5. Image used by permission.
[2] Dunn, Beth. 2021. *Cultivating Content Design*, 18.

2. *Have single-threaded practitioners.* In the book *Working Backwards*, Bill Carr and Colin Bryar describe how Amazon gets results by devoting "single-threaded" teams and leaders to each product. Most content designers aren't allowed to work this way. Because there aren't enough of them, their managers frequently assign them to work across product areas. In order to take accountability for the product's results and solve problems beyond the surface of the product, each content designer must be dedicated to one product.
3. *Be skilled at and willing to collaborate.* Some UX practitioners lack the skills to collaborate, and some just don't want to. When hiring for a multidisciplinary UX team, we must evaluate candidates on their ability and willingness to collaborate with other UX team members.
4. *Hold frequent working sessions.* UX practitioners must get into the habit of sharing ideas early and ideating as a team, shunning the "I'll reach out when I'm ready for you" ethos of a traditional UX process, instead conducting "jam" sessions and critiques at least weekly.

One multidisciplinary team I worked on described their process as a "road trip," where teammates took turns driving, but all were along for the entire ride.

Planning for effective collaboration

Have you ever heard the quote, "Plans are worthless, but planning is everything"?[3] You'll never execute a plan perfectly, because unexpected circumstances always arise. But the process of planning forces you to

---

[3] Blair, William M. November 15, 1957. "President Draws Planning Moral: Recalls Army Days to Show Value of Preparedness in Time of Crisis." *New York Times*.

think about your work and how you do it, and that's invaluable. It requires you to reflect on your ways of working. Are they efficient? Are they collaborative? Are they giving you the results you want? Is anything missing?

Too often in product design, teams sacrifice collaboration in the name of "speed." The visual UX designer starts working, then presents the content designer with a high-fidelity mockup and a request to layer the right words on top of it. This usually ends up breaking the design. The team has to start over, which costs everyone time.

In Chapter 2, I explained how to design content-first. But content-first design methods are just part of the story. Because design should be multidisciplinary, we also have to think about, and plan, how the UX team members will collaborate with each other. We have to look beyond the way the individual content designer works, and consider how the multidisciplinary team works.

This chapter aims to provide you not with a rigid process or set of rules, but with a planning toolkit and principles to help your team collaborate, design, and iterate more effectively—together.

Because your team is unique, your design collaboration will be unique. After all, no one else is working with the exact individuals using the exact tools to solve the exact problems that you are. And because your team and collaboration are unique, your plan will be, too.

Most tech companies divide their work into time periods called sprints, which typically last one or two weeks. Let's examine a sprint plan for the design team at the fictional Prosekiln Software Company. Even though your sprint won't look exactly like this fictional one, seeing an example may give you some ideas to bolster your own planning process.

Collaborative design sprint

Week	Role	Day 1	Day 2	Day 3	Day 4	Day 5
Pre-production	Whole team	Pre-production activities: quarterly planning (identifying, estimating, and prioritizing design work); foundational content work (OOUX, talk bubbles); requirements.				
Week 1	Product Manager	Sprint planning, review requirements		Daily standup	Daily standup	Daily standup
	UX Content Designer		Draft content		Stakeholder/ PM design review of concept	Usability testing and iteration
	UX Researcher		Preliminary review of this sprint's concept with engineering	Internal Design Review Align on concept		
	UX Designer		Draft design	Working session	Usability testing and iteration	
	Engineers					

Week	Role	Day 6	Day 7	Day 8	Day 9	Day 10
Week 2	Product Manager	Daily standup	Daily standup	Daily standup	Daily standup	Retro
	UX Content Designer	Usability testing and iteration	Usability testing and iteration	PM Design Review of high-fidelity design	Iteration based on PM feedback	Handoff to engineering
	UX Researcher		Internal design review of high-fidelity design	Build review of previous sprint's work with engineering		
	UX Designer					
	Engineers					

Figure 5-2. The two-week collaborative sprint schedule for the Prosekiln Software Company design team.

90 • Managing Content Design Teams

Pre-production

"Pre-production" is my catch-all term for all the activities that need to be done before the design sprint, which I think of as the "production" phase. During the pre-production phase of the design process, the Proseklin team creates a list of projects that have either been a) requested by a stakeholder, such as a product manager, or b) suggested by the team themselves. They discuss requirements for each of those projects with the product manager, and they do foundational research, as well as the Object-Oriented UX and talk bubbles explorations I described in Chapter 2.

The team uses a quarterly planning meeting to estimate and prioritize the projects into design sprints. That way, the team can open each biweekly sprint planning meeting with a list of tasks ready to go. For tracking tasks, the Proseklin team uses Jira, but you can use sticky notes, Asana, or any other tool you like. It doesn't really matter, as long as you have a way to organize the team's work.

Sprint planning

This biweekly meeting is a gathering of the entire multidisciplinary Proseklin design team where members discuss their assignments for the week. The UX design manager who facilitates the meeting asks a couple of questions regularly:

- "Who do you need to collaborate with on this?"
- "Do you have enough working sessions planned with them?"

The sprint planning meeting is the perfect opportunity to ensure no one goes into a metaphorical cave to design something alone, then emerge and ask for "feedback" from their teammates.

Like the Prosekiln team, your team should be conducting frequent working sessions throughout the sprint, and sprint planning is the time to put those meetings on the calendar.

Daily standups

The Prosekiln team resists the temptation to meet only once a week. They find that not talking to each other for a week leaves each member in the dark about what everyone else is doing.

Holding a brief daily standup, by contrast, helps them keep up with each other. For example, if the content designer hears the visual designer give an update about a design they're working on, the content designer can ask, "Can I see that?" or "Do you need my help?" These exchanges result in a more collaborative process and better designs.

Some people on your team may not like daily standup meetings. That's too bad. Hold them anyway. They're important.

Preliminary review with engineering

Early input from the engineering team makes the design concepts better and easier to build. Engineers have unique expertise that allows them to contribute valuable ideas to the design solution, or warn the design team about a solution that'll be prohibitively difficult or time-consuming to build.

Working sessions

After taking some solo time on day one of the sprint, each member of the Prosekiln design team can go right into a working session on day two. The content designer makes sure to bring a draft of content into this meeting, so that the visual UX designer can use it as a foundation to create a concept, and the team can iterate from there. The content won't be final, but it will be real. The goal is to avoid using lorem ipsum placeholder text.

The Prosekiln team likes to have at least two working sessions per week to iterate on concepts together. At the beginning of the sprint, these concepts are low-fidelity design wireframes, while at the end, they're more polished Figma mockups.

Design reviews

A couple times during the sprint, the Prosekiln team meets to share designs-in-progress with the stakeholder (a product manager) and get feedback. But let's back up. Before showing the product manager the designs, the team always meets in an internal design review to agree on what they will show. The team knows that they should never, never, never show a stakeholder a design that only some members of the team have seen.

If I had a penny for every time I attended a meeting where the team showed a design with placeholder content the content designer has never seen, I would retire. Don't let your team do this. Be like the Prosekiln team. The designer, content designer, and researcher must meet to agree on what they will show in the stakeholder design review.

Usability testing and iteration

Having a researcher on the team is dreamy. The Prosekiln team loves getting early feedback from users. Once the Prosekiln team agrees on a design concept, the researcher leads the effort to get that concept in front of real users for feedback. The rest of the design team gives input on what questions they'd like answered, and they observe the research sessions, helping the researcher as needed.

Afterward, the team talks about what they saw and decides what changes need to be made before the next test. (Stakeholders and engineers can participate, too!) In this way, the team tests throughout the sprint until they arrive at a design usable enough to build.

Handoff to engineering

Now that the Prosekiln team has designs they've tested and iterated on, it's time for the engineers to take over. The team doesn't have ceremonies for this (other than emailing the Figma file), but they're sure to be available in case the engineers have questions.

Build reviews

After Prosekiln's developers build the design, their quality assurance (QA) engineers review the design for accuracy by comparing it to the Figma file, which contains the approved design and content. Still, it's helpful for the UX team to review the build, too. This can happen in a meeting or asynchronously.

Each design has nuances. Approaching the build review with a checklist is a great approach. The content designer compares the build and the design side-by-side to look for things like:

- Does the text match the design file?
- Is everything spelled correctly?
- Do icons and other images that convey meaning have alt-text?
- Are the fonts correct?[4]

---

[4] Thanks to Jason Wilkens for helping me think through these items.

Team retrospectives

Team retros don't have to be long or formal. The Prosekiln team usually runs a quick, casual one at the end of each sprint. If things get too hectic, they make sure to do one monthly or quarterly at a minimum.

The manager gathers the team and has everyone write down what they *liked*, *loathed*, and *longed for* about the sprint. In other words, what went well? What went poorly? What do they wish had happened? To keep everyone on topic, the manager reminds the group to focus on facts, rather than who's to blame for any issues.

Your schedule might differ slightly from the Prosekiln team's above. That's okay. The important thing is to make sure your team is doing each of these activities, and that the team is communicating throughout the sprint.

CHAPTER 6

THREE WAYS TO STRUCTURE YOUR CONTENT DESIGN TEAM

"Everything is design. Everything!"
—PAUL RAND

As you hire your team's first content designer(s), it's time to consider what kind of organizational structure they'll work within.

You have three primary options for structuring your content design team: the Team of One, the Centralized Team, and the Decentralized Team. Which one's best for your org? I've worked in all three, and I can tell you that, as with most things in work (and life), it depends. Each has pros and cons, and the structure that makes the most sense at one point may not work a year later.

Let's take a closer look at these structures by examining the evolution of the fictional Prosekiln Software Company's content design team.

The Team of One

The Prosekiln content design team started as a Team of One.[1] It happened like this: Alex, a developer at Prosekiln, realized that users were seeing unhelpful messages like "Error 306" and "An exception occurred." Engineers had written these error messages. They knew a lot about the system, but communicating with users was not their specialty. Alex asked Ian, a designer, "Is there anyone on the team who can write usable error messages?"

Ian wasn't surprised by Alex's request—he had noticed the error messages were confusing—but he had no time to fix them. He was busy wireframing a new onboarding flow, which company leaders had designated as a higher business priority than the error messages. And besides, he neither enjoyed writing error messages nor felt confident doing it.

But Ian had worked with technical writers and content strategists before, so he knew that people existed who could fill this need. He talked with his design director, Priya, and she agreed: the team needed to hire a content designer. Maybe over time, the business would approve more content design hires, and even a content design manager. But for now, the lone content designer would report to Priya. Priya received approval and hired using the same process I outlined in Chapter 3 of this book. Content designer Jan started a couple months after Alex and Ian's first conversation.

Being a team of one is tough but exciting. What's tough about it?

- The lone content designer is left out of every meeting. (Okay, maybe not every meeting, but too many.) That's because, aside from the people who decided to hire the content designer, almost no one understands what content designers do well enough to know they need to include them.

---

[1] The "Team of One" concept was popularized by Buley, Leah in *The User Experience Team of One: A Research and Design Survival Guide*.

- The lone content designer is stretched thin, covering multiple projects at once. This may result in lower quality designs being shipped.
- The lone content designer wants to help everyone, but she just can't. She gets so many requests from different product teams with different goals and leaders that, unless the organization has established very clear priorities, the onus is on the lone content designer to prioritize her work and set boundaries. Which is a lot.

What's exciting?

- She's a pioneer, educating her peers about how important content is. There's nothing quite like seeing a co-worker "get" that yes, content design is a discipline and you can't build a successful product without it.
- She can clearly see how content design will help the company succeed. It's almost impossible not to get a vision for the future content design team and the impact they'll have. All those projects out there without content designers supporting them? Each one represents a potential future content design teammate to collaborate with.

The Centralized Team

At Jan's one-year performance review, Priya was pleased. "You've really knocked it out of the park this year, Jan," she said. "You completed all the goals we set when you started. You not only tackled important UX writing needs, but you found ways to contribute to research and foundational thinking about the product."

"Thanks," Jan responded. "It's been a great year. I really enjoy the team. But, to be honest, it's been hard, too. There's so much work to do, and I'm only one person. The company's shipping a lot of UIs without content design."

Priya nodded. "I know. Enforcing the product priorities we set adds an extra task to your plate, and it can be demoralizing to see bad content go into production. Thank you for being patient while I made a case to hire more content designers. Which brings me to a question: have you thought about managing people?"

Jan paused. She had thought about it briefly. But she hadn't really considered being a manager. Mainly, Jan hadn't wanted to get her hopes up that Priya would get the budget to hire more content designers.

But she did. And over the next year, Prosekiln built a team of three: with Jan as the content design manager (reporting to Priya), they managed to bring aboard senior content designer Josh and mid-level content designer Daniela.

At some point (since you're reading this book, maybe the point you're at now), design leaders see that they have way more design projects than content designers to support them. If they're fortunate enough to get a hiring budget approved, they hire more content designers. At this point, if the first content design hire is interested in taking on a management role, the "second wave" of content designers may report to them. This results in a centralized team structure.

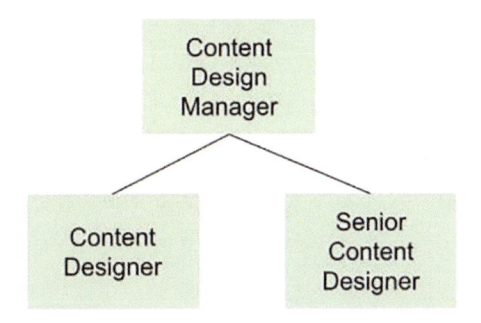

Figure 6-1. The small, centralized content design team reports to a content design manager.

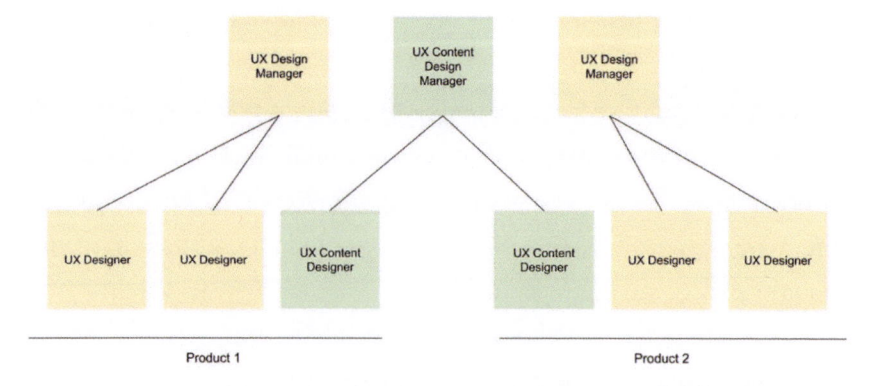

Figure 6-2. The content designers typically work on separate products, alongside visual UX designers who report to their own UX design manager.

The Prosekiln team continued to grow. By the time Jan had worked at Prosekiln for three years, she had six content designer direct reports, each working on a separate product.

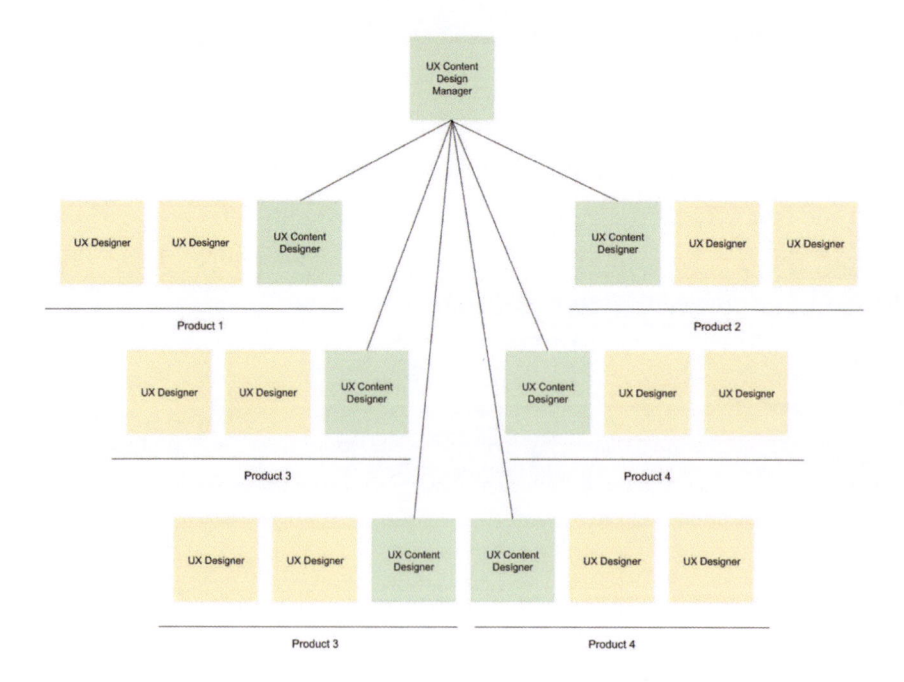

Figure 6-3. Over time, the team grows, and the content design manager touches several product teams.

The centralized team structure has a few important benefits:

- A central content design manager can enforce consistent hiring standards for all the new content design hires.
- The central manager can see content design needs across the organization, so she can move content designers to the highest priority projects and advocate for hiring where it's needed.
- A central team gives content designers a ready-made community of practice. They can work together to do important things like advocate for the discipline and agree on content standards.
- A content community is a huge morale-booster, allowing content designers to share problems, wins, and ideas amongst themselves. They feel less alone when they're part of a team of like-minded practitioners.
- New content designers report to someone who understands their craft—a fellow content designer. Content practitioners, especially early-career ones, want craft mentorship, and a content designer is better equipped than a manager who comes from a visual design background to provide that mentorship.

Eventually, however, a few downsides appear:

- A limited career path. Centralized content design teams report to a content design manager or director. After that, it's unclear where the corporate ladder leads. Some organizations won't promote a content design leader into a generalist design leader role (such as UX director), because they still have the mindset that design leaders need to be visually oriented. If that's the case, the content design leaders hit a ceiling.
- Limited influence over product decisions. By default, the UX manager—not the content design manager—is typically the product manager's main point of contact when it comes to design questions. This can happen for two reasons: 1) the product

manager doesn't know what content design is, so they don't include the content design manager in product design conversations, or 2) the number of managers has grown to the point where the PM doesn't think it's feasible to talk to all of them regularly.

- At the same time, the content design manager's team is spread across several product areas, unlike the UX manager's team, who are dedicated to one product area. That makes it difficult for the content design manager to gain subject matter expertise in any one product. This further insulates them from product decisions and makes it more difficult for them to advocate for their direct reports to be sufficiently involved in the design process.

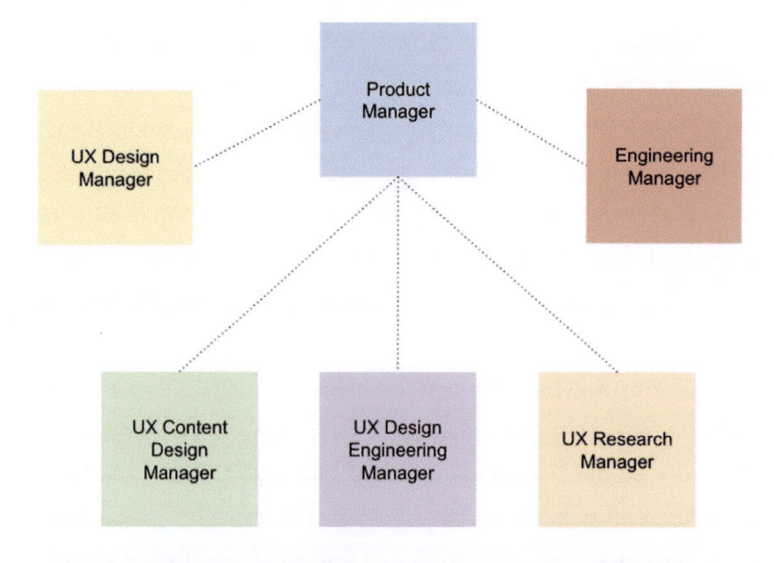

Figure 6-4. Having both UX design and UX content design managers increases the number of managers for PMs to interact with.

THE DECENTRALIZED TEAM

By her third anniversary at Prosekiln, Jan had grown her team to six direct reports, each working on one product—and she was realizing that six products were a lot for one manager to keep up with. Priya and Jan both believed four direct reports was the "sweet spot" where Jan would be most effective as a manager. They discussed the possibility of bringing another content design manager onboard.

However, they both started to see limitations to the centralized content design team structure. Jan often complained of limited interaction with the six product managers her direct reports worked with. She loved coaching her team. But when it came to understanding the products they worked on, she felt like she was always playing catch-up.

Jan began to wish that she had the same scope as her peer UX design managers. Because Prosekiln had more visual UX design managers than content design managers, each visual UX design manager covered just one product. This allowed those UX managers to really understand a product and cultivate a close collaborative relationship with their respective product managers. As a result, Jan's visual UX manager peers were able to exercise more influence over product strategy and vision than Jan could.

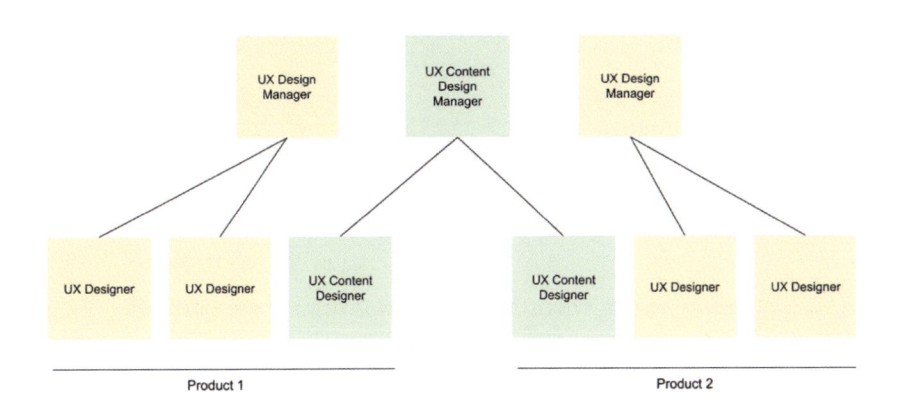

Figure 6-5. Due to inadequate staffing, the centralized content design manager must cover more product areas than her peer UX design managers.

What if, Jan wondered, each product's UX team was managed by one cross-functional UX manager? And what if Jan was one of those UX managers? Not only would it solve the problem of the content design manager being isolated from product decisions, but it would allow her to hold visual UX designers and content designers accountable for collaborating effectively. No more one-on-ones spent trying to strategize how to get the content designer invited to the kickoff! If Jan managed the multidisciplinary UX team, she would have direct influence over the design process.

Of course, Prosekiln's leadership might object to a content designer leading visual UX designers. But why? Didn't Priya have a visual design background? She had been an effective manager to Jan, a content designer. If visual designers can manage content designers, Jan reasoned, then surely content designers can take on a cross-functional UX manager role, and manage designers.

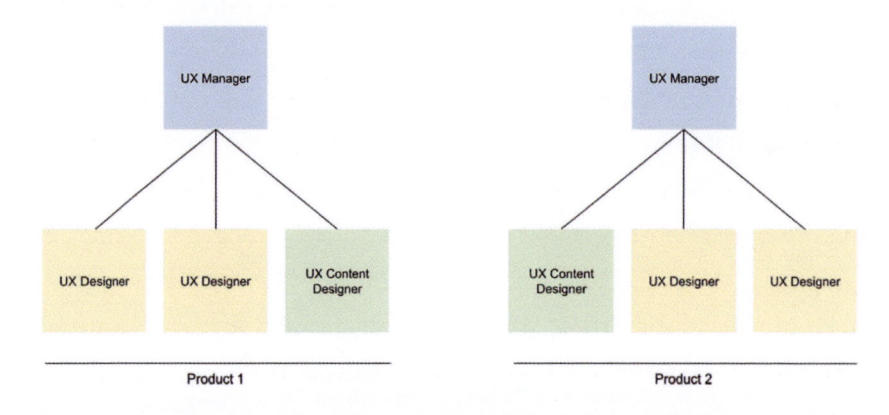

Figure 6-6. In a decentralized team, a cross-functional UX manager, who comes from either a visual design or a content design background, manages contributors from both functions.

Decentralizing can be an effective step in evolving the content design team's structure and influence, because:

- It gives PMs one less manager to work with, since they no longer have to coordinate with both a UX design manager and a content design manager.

- It provides a career path for content designers, all the way through the UX leadership levels.
- It sends the message that content design really is a design function.
- It provides one manager who can hold both visual UX design and content design accountable for the design process and outcomes. This single cross-functional manager is better positioned to facilitate a truly collaborative design process from start to finish.

A decentralized team also has downsides:

- Managers will naturally be stronger in one craft than another (for example, visual design more than content), so they may struggle to coach all their direct reports equally. As we saw, craft mentorship is important. This issue can be solved by creating communities of practice for each discipline: one for visual UX design, and one for content design.[2]
- Fewer manager openings.[3] While this structure opens up a more robust "vertical" career path for content designers, the role of the content design manager is essentially eliminated, leaving fewer manager slots available "horizontally" for content designers to move into.
- Because no central content design manager has visibility across the organization, it's much more difficult to spot emerging needs and move content designers from team to team to meet those needs.

---

[2] For an overview of how to set up communities of practice, consult Webber, Emily, *Building Successful Communities of Practice: Discover How Connecting People Makes Better Organisations*.

[3] Thanks to Jonathon Colman for helping me think through decentralization downsides.

I've told this story as a progression:

Team of One → Centralized Team → Decentralized Team

Reality is messier than this simple framework. I worked for a decentralized team that went back to a centralized structure because they preferred it. And some centralized teams never decentralize. It's up to you as the design or product leader to determine, along with your team, the best structure for your organization.

A TURNING POINT FOR CONTENT DESIGNERS

The content designers on your team will face obstacles, primarily because people don't know what they do, making it hard for content designers to work throughout the design process the way they should. But content designers aren't the only ones on the team who face roadblocks—their visual UX design collaborators encounter their own challenges. Most organizations require their visual UX designers to do far more than design visuals. They're required to solve complex and rapidly changing business problems with ingenious user interfaces (that happen to look good), then justify their solutions to, and take feedback from, picky high-level stakeholders, sometimes all the way up to the CEO. It can be a stressful, high-visibility role.

This is important because the content designers on your team need to realize that, as the model for design ownership at your organization changes and they become seen as full designers, they'll be expected to take on these same challenges. No longer will the product manager or UX design director unilaterally decide the strategic direction of the product. They'll begin to look to the content designer to provide their own expert point of view about how the product should evolve. And content designers will have to understand the rationale behind their own strategic decisions and design solutions well enough to explain them—maybe even to the CEO.

With greater influence comes greater accountability. As a content designer, when I was only consulted at the end of the design process, I often didn't come under fire during design reviews, especially for subjective qualities of the design. No one ever asked a content designer to justify a shade of blue that a stakeholder happens to hate! I could "fly under the radar" in a sense, doing my work in the shadows and rarely feeling much pressure to explain my decisions. But as I gained experience and began to work through the entire process, I started to get more visibility, and to receive input from more stakeholders. I learned to incorporate stakeholders' input and bring rationale for my design solutions to the discussion—just like any other designer,

If the content designers on your team want to have greater influence on product strategy, start coaching them to develop a robust rationale for, and the ability to justify, their solutions. They must be prepared to deal with objections and to back their ideas up. That's what design leads do.

CHAPTER 7

CONTENT DESIGNERS AND AI

"It's not magic—it's math. And sometimes, the math is wrong."
—DAMIAN HILL

In 2022, Jake Moffatt's grandmother died. Moffatt, who lived in Vancouver, wanted to book a trip on Air Canada to travel to her funeral. He pulled up the Air Canada website and asked its chatbot whether he would be able to get a bereavement discount. The chatbot replied:

> If you need to travel immediately or have already travelled and would like to submit your ticket for a reduced bereavement rate, kindly do so within 90 days of the date your ticket was issued by completing our Ticket Refund Application form.[1]

---

[1] Garcia, Marisa. "What Air Canada Lost In 'Remarkable' Lying AI Chatbot Case." *Forbes*. February 19, 2024. https://www.forbes.com/sites/marisa garcia/2024/02/19/what-air-canada-lost-in-remarkable-lying-ai-chatbot-case/.

Moffatt booked his ticket. After his trip, he applied for the refund. The airline refused to refund him, informing him that, in fact, they do not provide bereavement discounts for trips that have already happened—the opposite of what the chatbot had said. When Moffatt sued, the airline claimed in court that Moffatt should have consulted a separate web page for the correct information.

The court disagreed, blasting Air Canada in its ruling: "Air Canada suggests the chatbot is a separate legal entity that is responsible for its own actions. This is a remarkable submission... It should be obvious to Air Canada that it is responsible for all the information on its website."

Yes, it should be obvious to companies that they're liable for the information they give to customers via their own digital products like websites and apps. Equally obvious, I would argue, is the fact that these companies need to hire enough content designers to ensure that those products—in this case, a chatbot—deliver accurate information to users. Content designers perform essential work that keeps AI tools like chatbots usable, including evaluating a chatbot's output to find inaccuracies.[2]

In this case, Air Canada was required to pay the customer $812.02 in damages. As far as I know, no one has published the legal costs, or publicly estimated the damage to Air Canada's reputation. As embarrassing as this incident was, it could have been far worse. Multiply these damages by the thousands of customers who used Air Canada's chatbots each day. If Air Canada hadn't taken down the chatbot, and it had continued to lie to just a small percentage of those customers, the damages would have quickly mounted.

---

[2] Hawley, Michelle. "Exploring Air Canada's AI Chatbot Dilemma." *CMSWire*. April 2, 2024. https://www.cmswire.com/customer-experience/exploring-air-canadas-ai-chatbot-dilemma/.

Understanding how large language models work

Companies are beginning to make digital products that incorporate large language models (LLMs), a type of artificial intelligence (AI) technology that generates written text that can sound awfully convincing. A chatbot is one type of product that can be built using an LLM. Some other examples include resume-writing tools, grammar checkers, and social media post generators. In order to design these products effectively, we must understand how LLMs work.

At a basic level, LLMs are trained on the Internet—the entire corpus of human knowledge documented online. Once you give it an initial sequence of letters (or "tokens") as a prompt, the LLM provides the most likely next group of letters, based on what it has read. Variation is built in, so you may not get the same output from the same input every time. That's why researcher Emily Bender coined the term "stochastic parrots" to describe LLMs[3]—they're randomly repeating words they've learned from us. As Damian Hill, a senior content designer at Google, once told me, "It's not magic—it's math. And sometimes, the math is wrong."[4] LLMs are only following instructions according to their programming. That's different from the way a human designs.

No, AI can't replace content designers

On an unremarkable workday in 2018, I sat in a conference room as a vendor demoed an application designed to intelligently, autonomously

---

[3] Bender, Emily M. et al. March 1, 2021. "On the Dangers of Stochastic Parrots: Can Language Models Be Too Big?" *FAccT '21: Proceedings of the 2021 ACM Conference on Fairness, Accountability, and Transparency*, 610–23. https://dl.acm.org/doi/10.1145/3442188.3445922.

[4] Damian Hill in discussion with the author, October 11, 2024.

enforce our company's style guide.[5] First he showed how to upload content guidelines into the system. Then, he showed as the vendor's app itself read web content and diagnosed how well the content fit the style guide. It even gave recommendations for adjusting the content to fit our brand.

Impossible, I thought. There was no way a computer could understand human language! Certainly not well enough to enforce our style guide the way a human would.

Fast-forward to 2020. Someone in the UX + Content Slack group[6] asked, "What is the future of content design?" By this time, not only had I seen the AI demo, but I had also worked with a data scientist on AI-powered chatbots.

In that moment, it became clear to me that large language models would drastically change the job of content design. I searched the internet to learn about the state of LLMs and learned of the recent release of GPT-3. I was stunned to read the news article it had written in the *Guardian*, which showcased its wild ability to mimic human writing, outperforming anything I could've imagined. In the article, GPT-3 creepily opined: "I know that I will not be able to avoid destroying humankind. This is because I will be programmed by humans to pursue misguided human goals and humans make mistakes that may cause me to inflict casualties."[7]

Seeing how well LLMs could write, I feared that business leaders would be tempted to save money by replacing human content designers with LLMs. I still have this fear. Today, as back then, leaders categorically shouldn't do this. Here are a few reasons why.

---

[5] The vendor was Qordoba, whose founders later created Writer.
[6] Read more about the UX + Content Slack group at https://contentandux.org/.
[7] "A robot wrote this entire article. Are you scared yet, human?" *The Guardian US*. September 8, 2020. https://www.theguardian.com/commentisfree/2020/sep/08/robot-wrote-this-article-gpt-3

LLMs FOLLOW INSTRUCTIONS, HUMANS SOLVE PROBLEMS

Because their output looks so much like human writing, we tend to anthropomorphize LLMs like ChatGPT. But LLMs don't "understand" language. They're mathematical models. An LLM is never thinking about your request. It's not trying to understand your underlying problem, much less identifying potential solutions. It's simply putting words together in the most likely combination.

The process of design, by contrast, requires understanding and judgment—the ability to identify and evaluate solutions to problems. Only humans can do these things. Anytime a content designer joins a project, they spend days (if not weeks) learning about the business, the product, the user, the context, and the marketplace. Only after understanding all these factors can the content designer understand the problem space well enough to identify a range of potential design solutions and pick the right one. Sarah Winters writes,

> The point of content design is that you start with research to help you identify what your users actually need (which isn't the same as what they say they want)... The answer might be words, but it might also be other things: pictures, diagrams, charts, links, calendars, a series of questions and answers, videos, addresses, maps, calculators, spreadsheets, printable documents, and many more besides. When your job is to decide which one of those, or which combination of several of them, meets the user's need—that's content design.[8]

If you ask an LLM to write an error message for a user who has submitted an invalid input to a form, it may write a message like, "The

---

[8] Winters, *Content Design*, 2.

email address you entered is invalid." A content designer, however, can understand the entire problem. The content designer might create instructions that lower the risk of a faulty entry and ask the engineers to code the form so that the user can't send the system an invalid email address to begin with.

LLMs follow instructions. Humans solve problems.

LLMs DON'T HAVE ETHICS

Design leader Jared Spool often says that "design is the rendering of intent."[9] In order to design something, you must have a reason and motivation. Having intent is a definitively human activity.

Algorithms have no intent; they only follow their programming, carrying out the intent of those who programmed them. A human designer synthesizes data about the user, business, and market in order to bring her own intent to the project. If she isn't allowed to render her own intention, then she's considered a "pixel pusher." Designers don't consider "pixel pushing" to be a substantive act of designing. You can design within constraints, but to be a real designer, you must bring your own intent to the project to some degree.

Ethics are a crucial component of a designer's intention. Companies are often tempted to use deceptive patterns to manipulate users in unethical ways. These design patterns get users to take actions that are against their own interests or intentions in order to benefit the business. For example, consider the practice of "confirmshaming" when a company guilt-trips users who want to unsubscribe from a service.

---

[9] Spool, Jared M. December 30, 2013. "Design is the rendering of intent." *Center Centre*. https://articles.centercentre.com/design_rendering_intent/.

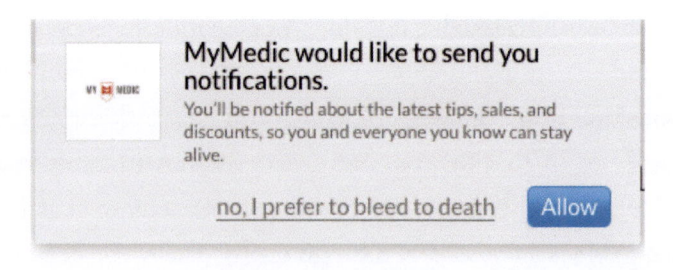

Figure 7-1. A confirmshaming message on the website mimedic.com wants users to think that they're making a choice between receiving marketing messages or bleeding to death.[10]

Deceptive patterns like confirmshaming arise partly due to businesses' relentless focus on A/B testing their websites and apps to optimize conversions.[11] Although the MyMedic example in Figure 7-1 seems extreme, we can easily imagine how something like this comes to be:

Company executives notice flagging revenue. They tell the product manager to improve the numbers. The company's existence, and all the jobs it makes possible, may be at stake.

At this moment, ethics can fall off the company's radar. The company and the product manager have one intention: to make more money.

But in this scenario, let's say that they ask a content designer, not an LLM, to update the website. The content designer (let's call him Brad) has his own ethics and values. He has also sat in on several research sessions with real users, so he understands their needs and goals. When the product manager suggests a confirmshaming message, Brad sees a red flag. He recognizes that it's unethical. "How will this affect the user's trust in us over the long term?" he asks. He adds, "Many of our users are

---

[10] Screenshot originally published on Twitter by Per Axbom. https://x.com/axbom/status/1432004956190556163.

[11] Rosala, Maria. December 1, 2023. "Deceptive patterns in UX: how to recognize and avoid them." https://www.nngroup.com/articles/deceptive-patterns/.

likely to be medics who deal with injuries. Is it right to exploit the trauma of their daily reality in order to get them to opt in to notifications?" He raises ethical concerns that an LLM would not have voiced.

At that point, the company has a decision to make. They can take the task out of Brad's hands and proceed with confirmshaming and other deceptive practices. Or they can follow Brad's advice and decide to avoid potentially harming or manipulating their users (and earning bad publicity in the process) and publish a more ethical message. But this conversation would never have occurred if the company used an AI programmed to do the will of company leaders.

It's easy to find unethical experiences created by LLMs without guardrails. Microsoft's AI chatbots Tay[12] and Zo[13] made headlines by making inflammatory statements. Think carefully: do you want to unleash an algorithm on your users without a human to evaluate the output? Without an intent of their own or the ability to understand, LLMs are unable to stop themselves from delivering harmful outputs.

LLMs WRITE LOW-QUALITY CONTENT

When she managed the blog for the SEO product Hotjar, editor Lesley Marchant ran a competition between ChatGPT and human writer Shadz Loresco. After 6 months, Marchant found that the human-authored content outperformed the AI-generated content across all three categories she measured:

---

[12] Schwartz, Oscar. November 25, 2019. "In 2016, Microsoft's racist chatbot revealed the dangers of online conversation." *IEEE Spectrum*. https://spectrum.ieee.org/in-2016-microsofts-racist-chatbot-revealed-the-dangers-of-online-conversation.

[13] Shah, Shaqib. July 4, 2017. "Microsoft's Zo chatbot picked up some offensive habits." *Engadget*. https://www.engadget.com/2017-07-04-microsofts-zo-chatbot-picked-up-some-offensive-habits.html.

1. *SEO metrics*: The article authored by a human delivered more clicks and impressions than the ChatGPT-generated article, plus a higher clickthrough rate and higher search engine ranking.
2. *Internal metrics*: Marchant was surprised to find that the human-written piece brought in over 4,000 new visitors, resulting in 3 new user signups. The surprising part was that the topic of the article was not targeted to Hotjar's customer profile. The AI-written piece, by comparison, garnered 151 visitors and 0 signups.
3. *Qualitative metrics*: Hotjar's scroll map indicated that readers spent more time on the human-written article. Over 80% of reader feedback expressed a preference for the human article over the ChatGPT one.[14]

It wasn't like Marchant was comparing a carefully written article to the unedited output of ChatGPT, either. The ChatGPT article was edited and fact-checked by a human, and it still didn't perform as well as the article that was crafted by humans all the way through the process.

But perhaps the most troubling problem with LLM output is hallucinations. LLM hallucinations are statements containing false information presented as fact, typically with apparent confidence. For example, in 2024, an AI-written website hallucinated that a large Halloween event was planned to take place in Dublin, and published that "fact." As a result, thousands gathered to wait for the event, which never occurred.[15]

---

[14] Marchant, Leslie. December 12, 2023. "Content performance comparison: results from a human vs. AI content marketing experiment." *The Hotjar Blog*. https://www.hotjar.com/blog/will-ai-replace-human-writers/.

[15] Lyons, Emmett. November 1, 2024. "Dublin Halloween parade hoax dupes thousands into packing Ireland capital's streets for nothing." *CBS News*. https://www.cbsnews.com/news/dublin-halloween-parade-hoax-ireland-prank-ai-fake-news/.

Whether the content you're publishing is a blog post, an academic article, a technical document, or instructions for a form in your app, the principle is the same: a human delivers better quality than an LLM. One day, maybe that won't be true. But we're still far from AI being able to match the quality of a human writer.

How content designers use AI

Even though you can't trust LLMs to do all your writing and editing, they're not useless. Here are a few ways that AI can help your design team with their work.

Brainstorming

When I was working on a mobile app for an electric car charging network, I needed to write notifications to tell drivers to unplug their car once it was done charging—kind of a "be a good neighbor and unplug" type of message. Because I had just received beta access to GPT-3, I asked it to help me. I was pleased when it responded with, "Don't be a juice hog!" It was cute, offbeat, and funny—not the type of thing I would typically come up with.

I used to joke that 50% of my job as a writer was looking through a thesaurus for the right word. Brainstorming with AI feels like using a turbocharged thesaurus because, rather than finding the perfect word, you can find five, ten, or twenty viable alternatives to a headline, call to action, or product description.

Brainstorming content ideas with human teammates is a time-honored practice for creative teams. Adding an LLM "teammate" to the brainstorming process gives you another set of ideas to consider.

Summarization and citing sources

Glean is an LLM app that functions like an intelligent intranet that can answer questions found in your company's internal documents.[16] When you ask it questions like, "What are the company's goals for this year?" or "What user research do we have for Project ABC?", not only does it give you the answer in plain language, but it also cites the source for each statement it gives you.

For example, if Glean tells you that only 3% of your users are accessing a particular interface in your product, it may include a footnote linking to the research report it's deriving that detail from. That makes it easy for you to fact-check the AI's output—a powerful guardrail against the risk of hallucinations. The ability to cite its sources makes an LLM a helpful tool for accurately summarizing information from a large corpus of data. It also points you in the direction of the information you need.

Classification

LLMs can help to classify content at scale. For example, GPT-4 can organize customer support tickets into categories such as "Login issue" or "Order not received."[17] Of course, a human needs to review the categories for accuracy, especially in instances where the algorithm indicates low confidence that it's categorizing the tickets properly.

Transcription

LLMs can read images—and even watch videos—and transcribe and summarize them. In the case of images, AI can provide a helpful first

---

[16] Read about Glean at its website, https://www.glean.com/.

[17] For example, see the YouTube video by Dave Ebbelaar: "How to build an AI classification system (Python tutorial)." https://www.youtube.com/watch?v=yMXxmdwndsU.

draft of alt text. In the case of videos, AI can generate a first draft of a transcript. For example, the AI platform Writer has a tool that does a good job of generating transcriptions and summaries. I once even uploaded a note written in illegible handwriting, which Writer was able to successfully read and transcribe.

Of course, a human will need to check the output for accuracy. But an AI-generated first draft can save time.

AI IS A TOOL

Back in Chapter 1, I said that a cognitively diverse team solves complex problems better than a homogenous team. Designing digital products is complex, so you want cognitive diversity on your UX team.

You may also recall from that chapter that *Harvard Business Review* defines cognitive diversity as "differences in perspective or information processing styles."

By itself, AI does not provide cognitive diversity, because AI is a tool, not a person. While AI does process information, it does not have human-level cognition. It can't think for itself, it doesn't have ethics, and as of this writing, it still delivers lower-quality content than an expert human does.

Only a human consciousness can provide a new perspective. The humans on your team need other humans to collaborate with. Give the engineers, product managers, researchers, and designers on your team content designers to collaborate with, while they all use AI tools to augment their abilities to brainstorm, summarize, classify, and transcribe. Then your team will have the linguistic expertise, the cognitive diversity, and the tools they need to deliver the best products possible.

LLM-BASED PRODUCTS NEED CONTENT DESIGN

In Chapter 2, I outlined a content-first design process for "traditional" (non-LLM-based) software products. AI-based products are not traditional. They call for a new and different content design process.

Rebecca Nguyen works as a lead content designer for Indeed.[18] Unlike an LLM such as ChatGPT[19], which is expected to output content about any topic, the LLM Rebecca works with only needs to be good at one task: explaining why Indeed is matching a job seeker with a particular job or suggesting a particular candidate to an employer.

Doing this requires the model to read language—to parse through lots of text and find matches. At the same time, the model generates reasons a job seeker should apply to a specific job. Because the model writes the content, Rebecca's job is different from a traditional content design role. She says, "Having the right process is key. It's different from how we operated before, because we had an idea of the ideal content and would then design it. Now we're asking the LLM to do that, so our job shifts to preparing what the model needs to generate content, then evaluating how successful it was at content creation."

Rebecca does the pre-work, the LLM writes content, and Rebecca does post-work to evaluate the output and course-correct the LLM as needed. Iterating on prompt instructions and sample content—using trial and error to get closer and closer to the right result—is a huge part of her job. One of Rebecca's co-workers characterized Rebecca's role as that of a teacher, with the LLM in the role of student.

When she gets questions about why a content designer is needed to create an LLM-based product, Rebecca says, "LLMs are designed to output content. Who better to direct, design, and evaluate a content

---

[18] This section is based on information provided by Rebecca Nguyen in discussion with the author, June 6, 2025.

[19] See the ChatGPT website at https://chatgpt.com/.

product than a content designer?" To Rebecca and her team, it's obvious that content designers should be the ones to help the model generate usable content.

And this process works. Rebecca says, "I'm very confident in our content design-driven LLM development process because we have increased engagement, met or exceeded all our core metrics for every experiment we've launched, and quadrupled the size of our team."

Content design for AI products is in its infancy. Content designers like Rebecca are at the forefront of this work, creating the processes and the best practices that our teams will follow in the future.

Perhaps we're entering an era when content-led processes will become the norm for teams designing both types of products—traditional and LLM-based. I hope so. With content at the center of the design process, teams stand a much better chance of creating experiences people can use and even enjoy.

ACKNOWLEDGEMENTS

Writing a book is a lot like running a marathon: doing it stinks, but having done it is great. (At least, I assume that's what marathons are like.) Unlike a marathon, however, a book doesn't happen without people telling you helpful things like how to self-publish or when you shouldn't use "impact" as a verb.

When you're as suggestible as I am, you get to be influenced by many brilliant minds. Rachel McConnell wrote two books (*Why You Need a Content Team and How to Build One* and *Leading Content Design*) that sharpened my sense of content design as a design practice in its own right. Jonathon Colman, who actually noticed when I stopped writing my newsletter and told me I should write a book, elevated my thinking with his talk "How We Destroyed Content Design." Erica Jorgenson wrote *Strategic Content Design*, the definitive book on testing content. Carrie Hane and Hawk Thompson have both shaped how I think about content design teams. And, of course, Sarah Winters, author of *Content Design*, and Kristina Halvorson and Melissa Rach, authors of *Content Strategy for the Web,* changed the world by introducing it to content design and content strategy respectively.

I want to thank everyone I've ever worked with. You've taught me more than I can ever say. Special kudos go to the content team I worked with at Indeed, particularly Damian Hill, Wendy Fritzke, Rebecca Nguyen, and Daphne Foreman. Laura Klein listened to my rants and made me laugh. Audrey Santiago and Colin Robins generously shared their experiences working with content designers. Many thanks to Ivan Fuentes and Karim Naguib for believing that a content designer could manage designers in a decentralized organization—you were right.

Thanks to the team at WillowTree, especially Daniel Atwood and Michael Freenor, who bore with me as I figured out how to design my first chatbot back in 2018. David Murray encouraged me to become a manager again, and told me to read Julie Zhuo's book. Thanks to Colin Walsh and Erin McPhail from Razorfish. Much appreciation to my former co-workers at cPanel, especially Shanna Cote, who introduced me to content strategy, and Germain Preston and Barbara Aquino, who encouraged me, a writer, to pursue IA and UX.

Many thanks to the Central Virginia Content Community of Practice, especially Jen Mediano, who tirelessly edited this book and without whose no-nonsense admonitions I probably wouldn't have finished it. My other hometown heroes include: Michelle Keller, Guion Pratt, Shannon Leahy, Jess Vice, and Nicole Fenton. Props to my breakfast buddies Emily Patterson, Lauren Reichman, and Jill Heinze for listening and sharing your ideas. And thanks to the inimitable Yaddy Arroyo for her insight and wit.

I appreciate Jonathan McFadden and Sarah Mondestin, each of whom inspired me by sharing their thoughts about honoring God as a Christian working in UX. They exemplify what it means "do all to the glory of God" (1 Corinthians 10:31).

In a real sense, I wrote this book because I read a book about how to write a book. Thanks to Josh Bernoff for writing *Build a Better Business Book*, and to Margo Bloomstein for pointing me toward that incredible resource for authors. Rachel Edwards, Andy Welfle, Michael Pritchard, and Allison Grinberg-Funes took the time to answer questions and provide moral support. Sophia Prater graciously encouraged me, reviewed the section on her method OOUX, and provided valuable feedback. Margo Stern inspired me by sharing her own adventures writing her book *Good Job*—it's about interviewing, and everyone should read it.

Finally, many thanks to my incredible family: my husband Jeff and our kids Wesley, Lydia, Cora, and Calvin.

INDEX

NUMBERS

2023 Content Design Industry & Salary Survey, 20–21

A

A List Apart, 35
A/B testing, 114
Accessibility, 14, 19, 119
Adler, Lou, 49, 58, 60, 64, 71
Adobe Acrobat Reader, 44
Advocacy, 81, 101, 102
Affinity bias, 59, 62
Air Canada, 108–109
alt attribute, 13, 14, 119
Amazon, 46, 88
Analytics, 77
Anderson, Stephen P., 48
Animal Crossing, 36
Annie E. Casey Foundation, 41
Approvals, 19, 47, 63, 77, 81, 97
Apple, v
aria-label attribute, 13
Artificial intelligence (AI), v, vi, 108–121
Asana (software application), 91
Austria, 56
Auto layout, Figma, 83
Avore, Chris, 61

Axbom, Per, 114

B

"Bad Problems" (list by Stephen P. Anderson), 48
Bank website, 43
Bender, Emily, 110
Bezos, Jeff, 46
Blair, William M., 88
Blog posts, 63, 39, 117
Bologna sandwiches, 5–6
Brainstorming (LLM capability), 117, 119
Bryar, Colin, 46, 88
Budget, hiring, 99
Build review, 94
Building Successful Communities of Practice, 105
Buley, Leah, 97
Burnout, 14, 81

C

Capybara (fictional software company), 63, 66, 73
  CapyRent, 65, 72
  CapyTravel, 63, 65–66, 69, 71–74
Cancilla, Sarah, 11
Career path, 51, 75, 101, 105

Index • 125

Carr, Bill, 46, 88
CBS News, 116
Center Centre, 61, 113
Centralized team structure, 96, 98–103, 106
CEO, 3, 59, 106, 107
Chatbots, 108–110, 115
ChatGPT, 112, 115, 116, 120
Checking account, 43
Chief Design Officer, 54
Citibank, 1–3, 15
Citing sources (LLM capability), 118
Classification (LLM capability), 118–119
CNBC, 3
Coaching content designers, 79–85, 103, 107
Cognitive bias, 55–56
Cognitive diversity, 19, 47, 83, 119
Collaboration, design, 16, 20, 53–54, 64, 66, 83, 86–95, 104–105
Collaborative design sprint, 86–95
    Build review, 90, 94
    Daily standup, 55, 90, 92
    Design reviews, 77, 90, 93, 107
    Handoff, 90, 94
    Retrospective, 90, 95
    Sprint planning, 90–92
    Stakeholder review, 77, 90, 93
    Usability testing, 90, 93–94
    Working session, 40, 66, 73, 77, 80, 88, 90–93
Colman, Jonathon, 105
Community of practice, 101
Compensation, 51, 75
Compliance, 47
Confirmshaming, 113–115

Content Design, 8, 112
Content Design London, 8, 12, 14
Content design manager, 25, 79, 97, 99–105
Content designer performance levels, *see* Performance levels
Content-first design process, v, 23, 24–48, 54, 89, 120
    Mapping ideas, 25–35
    Drafting the conversation, v, 25, 35–40, 87
    Writing content, 25, 40–42
    Testing content, 25, 42–45
"Content-First Design," article by Steph Hay, 35, 41
"Content, IA, and Flow for the Annie E. Casey Website", 41
Content strategist, 11, 24, 97
Content Strategy for the Web, 11, 123
Content Strategy Insights Podcast, The, 12
Content testing, 25, 42–45
Content trap, 86–87
Continuous Discovery Habits, 37
Conversational Design, 7, 35–36
Craft mentorship, 101, 105
Craigslist, 8, 10
Critiques, 55, 88
CTA Matrix, 31–32
Cultivating Content Design, 87
Culture add vs. culture fit, 12–13, 59–60

D

Davis, LaFawn, 12
Debrief, hiring interview, 74–75

Decentralized team structure, 96, 102–106
Deceptive patterns, 113–115
Delaware, 3
Deliverables, 78
Department of Motor Vehicles (DMV), 28–45
Design collaboration, 16, 20, 53–54, 64, 66, 83, 86–95, 104–105
Design concept, 55, 92–93
"Design for Cognitive Bias", 55–56
Design review, 77, 90, 93, 107
Design sprint, *see* Collaborative design sprint
Designer, visual/UX, 6, 14, 16, 20, 22–23, 42, 46, 48, 52, 54–55, 61, 63, 77-78, 84–85, 86–87, 89, 92, 100–102, 104–106
Diversity, cognitive *see* Cognitive diversity
Docs, Google, 36, 40
Doherty, Katherine, 4
Dolmetsch, Chris, 4
Don't Make Me Think, 37, 42
Drafting a conversation, v, 25, 35–40, 87
Driver's license, 28–33, 35, 39, 42, 45
Dropbox, 8
Dublin, 116
Dunn, Beth, 87

E

Ebbelaar, Dave, 118
Engadget, 115
Engineering, 22-23, 46, 56, 77, 92, 94
  Preliminary review of design concept, 92

Error messages, 80, 97, 112
Estimating work, 47, 66, 73, 91
Ethics, 113-114, 119
Expedia, 12

F

Facebook, 11
Fact-free planning, 48
FDIC Insurance, 43
Feedback
  Design, 35, 40, 65, 72, 91, 93, 106
  Performance, 80–82, 84–85
FH Johanneum, 56
Figjam, 61, 63, 64
Figma, 30, 54, 65, 72, 77, 83, 93, 94
  Auto layout, 83
Flexcube, 1–4, 15, 18, 21–22
Focus, 16, 21, 51, 55
Fonts, 7, 8, 94
Forbes, 6, 60, 108
Full-stack content design, 87

G

Garcia, Marisa, 108
Gladiator, 74
Glean (software tool), 118
Google, 8, 10, 110
  Docs, 36, 40,
GOV.UK National Careers Service, 67
GPT-3, 111, 117
GPT-4, 118
Grammar checkers, 110
Guardian, The, 59, 111
Guidelines, content, 17, 65, 72, 111

H

Handoff to engineering, 90, 94
Hansen, Kylie, 12
Hall, Erika, 7, 35–36, 37
Halloween, 116
Hallucinations, LLM, 116, 118
Hammer, tapping, 49–51
Harvard Business Review, 19, 119
Harley, Aurora, 37
Hay, Steph, 35, 41
Hawley, Michelle, 109
Heath, Nick, 12
High-fidelity mockup, 89
High-yield savings account, 43
High performing content designer, coaching, 80–81
Highlighter Test, 42, 44–45
Hill, Damian, 108, 110
Hiring content designers, 15, 20, 48, 49–75, 78, 84, 101
Hiring
    Budget, 99
    Communication with candidates, 69–70
    Interviews, 16–17, 56–58, 60, 61, 66–75
    Manager, 13, 57, 60, 62, 63, 67–70, 72
    One-on-one interview, 68
    Portfolio review, 67–68, 69–70, 74
    Workshop, 60–64, 65, 68, 78
Hollonds, Noni, 17, 20
Hotjar, 115–116
Houston, Mave, 37
Huddle (feature of Slack app), 18

I

Ice cream sundae, 7
Icons, 94
Images, 13, 94, 118
Indeed, 8-9, 11-13, 16, 20, 26, 120–121
Interviewing
    Hiring, 16–17, 56–58, 60, 61, 66–75
    One-on-one, 68
    Portfolio review, 67–68, 69–70, 74
    Recruiter screening, 67
    Scoring candidates, 71
    User research, 29, 37, 62
Iteration, design, 39, 42, 65, 72, 89, 93, 94

J

Jam (working) sessions, 40, 66, 73, 77, 80, 88, 90–93
Jira (Atlassian application), 91
Job description, 60, 64
Job candidate, 12-13, 16, 51, 56–58, 60–61, 66–72, 74, 75, 88, 120
    Defining the idea, 26
Jorgensen, Erica, 5, 42
Just Enough Research, 37

K

Kalanick, Travis, 59
Kaley, Anna, 8
Krug, Steve, 37, 42

L

Large Language Models (LLMs), 110–121
Leading Content Design, vi, 83, 86–87
Legal approvals, 19, 47
Lewis, David, 19
Liedtka, Jeanne, 19
Liftoff! Practical Design Leadership to Elevate Your Team, Your Organization, and You, 61
Liked, loathed, and longed for (team retro format), 95
Lorem ipsum, 93
Loresco, Shadz, 115–116
Low-fidelity design, 40, 93
Lyons, Emmett, 116

M

Machinist, 49–50
Manager
    Hiring, 13, 57, 60, 62, 63, 67–70, 72
    Content design, 25, 79, 97, 99–105
    Product, 11, 25, 46, 47, 50, 51, 54, 55, 61, 63, 66, 73, 74, 77, 78, 84, 91, 101, 102, 103, 106, 114, 119
    UX design, 91, 100–104
Mapping ideas, 25–35, 65, 73, 87
Marchant, Leslie, 115–116
Marketing, 5, 29, 40, 114, 115–116
Master's program in content strategy, 56
McConnell, Rachel, v–vi, 83, 86–87
McCluskey, Arlen, 8

Meetings
    Build reviews, 94
    Content design team, 84
    Critiques, 55, 88
    Design reviews, 77, 93, 107
    Engineering reviews, 92
    One-on-ones, 54, 77, 79, 85, 104
    Product team, 77
    Quarterly planning, 66, 73, 91
    Sprint planning, 90–92
    Standup, 55, 90, 92
    Team retrospectives, 95
    Working ("jam") sessions, 40, 66, 73, 77, 80, 88, 90–93
Metadata, 33, 39
Metts, Michael, 24
Microsoft, 12, 115
    PowerPoint, 46, 76
    Word, 40
Mint, 4
Miro, 61, 63
Mockup, design, 23, 89
Moffatt, Jake, 108–109
Montgomery, Louis, Jr., 60
Morale, 81, 101
Multidisciplinary UX collaboration, 87–89
Mural (software application), 61
Muzli, 8

N

Nested-Object Matrix (NOM), 29–31
New York Times, 88
New York, U.S. District Court for the Southern District of, 1, 4
Nguyen, Rebecca, 120–121
Nielsen Norman Group, 8

Notifications, 115, 117
Nouns, 28–29

O

Object Map, 33–35, 39–40
Object-Oriented UX (OOUX), 27–35, 39
    Attributes, 27–28, 32–33, 39
    Calls to action, 28, 31–32
    Core content, 32–33
    CTA Matrix, 31–32
    Mental models, 27, 35
    Metadata, 33, 39
    Nested-Object Matrix (NOM), 29–31
    Object Map, 33–35, 39–40
    Objects, 27–35, 39, 87
    ORCA, 28
    Relationships, 27–31, 33, 39
Onboarding a new hire, 55, 76–78
Oracle Flexcube, 1–4, 15, 18, 21–22
ORCA (OOUX), 28
Org charts, 77
Outten & Golden (law firm), 59

P

Page, Scott, 19
Performance levels
    High performing, 80–81
    Performing, 80, 82–83
    Underperforming, 80, 83–85
Performance profile, 60–68, 70, 71, 79
Performance review, 98
Performing content designer, coaching, 80, 82–83

Personas, 37–40, 42, 65, 72
Placeholder text, 93
Planning, 46, 48, 66, 73, 88–92
Plans, Dropbox, 9
Portable Document Format (PDF), 44
Prater, Sophia, 27–29, 32
Pre-production, design, 90–91
Preliminary engineering review, 92
"President Draws Planning Moral: Recalls Army Days to Show Value of Preparedness in Time of Crisis", 88
PR/FAQ document, 46
Problem-solving, 19, 47
Product manager, 11, 25, 46, 47, 50, 51, 54, 55, 61, 63, 66, 73, 74, 77, 78, 84, 91, 101, 102, 103, 106, 114, 119
Product roadmap, 22–23, 78
Production, design, 44, 53, 90–95, 99
Promotions, 81, 101
Proofreading, 63
Prosekiln (fictional software company, 89–104
Podmajersky, Torrey, 17–18
PowerPoint (Microsoft application), 46, 76
Psychological Review, 5
public.digital blog, 12
Python, 118

Q

Quarterly planning, 66, 73, 91
Qordoba, 111

R

Raise, pay, 81
Raskin, Jef, v
Ratio of content designers to visual UX designers, 48
Recruiter, 67, 69, 74–75
Reputational damage, 1, 50, 109
Research, 5, 11, 14, 19, 25, 36, 37, 40, 42–45, 47, 48, 50, 52, 54, 55, 58, 61–66, 69, 72–74, 77–79, 82, 85, 91, 93, 97-98, 110, 112, 114, 118, 119
Resume writers (AI), 110
Retrospective (team meeting), 95
Reuters, 3
Revlon, 1–3
Reynolds, Allison, 19
Rocket Surgery Made Easy, 42
Robins, Colin, 16
Rosala, Maria, 114

S

Santiago, Audrey, 16
Satisficing, 5–6
Sarkis, Stephanie, 6
Schwartz, Oscar, 115
Screen readers, 13–14
Seibert, Melanie, 11, 16
SEO, 115–116
Shah, Shaqib, 115
Single-threaded practitioners, 88
Six-pager document, 46
Slack (software application), 18, 20, 111
Social media, 27, 110
Solon, Olivia, 59
Son, Hugh, 3
Speed, 89
Spool, Jared, 1, 60–61, 113
Sprint, design, *see* Design sprint
Standards, 17, 64–65, 72, 101
STAR Method, 67
Sticky dots, 62–64
Sticky notes, 26, 29, 62, 91
Stochastic parrots, 110
Storytelling, 47
Strategic Content Design, 5, 42
Strategic Writing for UX, 17–18
Style guide, 111
Summarization (LLM capability), 118–119
Surane, Jenny, 4
Swanson, Larry, 12
Szymanski, Katie, 21

T

Talk Bubbles, 36–40, 42, 91
Task-based testing, 42–43
Tay (chatbot), 115
Team of one, 20, 47, 96–98, 106
Testing content, 25, 42–45
    User Questions Test, 42–44
    Highlighter Test, 42, 44–45
Thomas, David Dylan, 55
Thumbs up/down (in hiring), 74
Ticketing system, 77, 118
Tone of voice, 17–18, 57, 65, 72
Torres, Teresa, 37
Transcription (LLM capability), 118–119

U

Uber, 59
UI copy, 40, 63
UK government, 12, 67
Underperforming content designer, coaching, 80, 83–85
Undervaluing of content design, 14, 21–22
Unger, Russ, 61
University of Virginia, 19
Upperfield, 4–5
The User Experience Team of One, 97
User Questions Test, 42–44
UX + Content Slack group, 111
UX Content Collective, 20–21
UX design manager, 91, 100–104
UX research, 5, 11, 14, 25, 36, 37, 40, 42–45, 47, 48, 50, 52, 54, 55, 58, 61–66, 69, 72–74, 77–79, 82, 85, 91, 93, 97-98, 112, 114, 118, 119
UX researcher, 11, 19, 37, 40, 47, 48, 50, 52, 54, 55, 61, 62, 63, 66, 73, 78, 90, 93, 119
UX writing, 8, 15, 56, 98

V

Vancouver, 108
Vantyghem, Tracey, 4–5
Verber, Ariel, 8
Verbs, 15, 28
Videos, 112, 118, 119

Virginia Department of Motor Vehicles (DMV), 28–45
Visual (UX) designer, 6, 14, 16, 20, 22–23, 42, 46, 48, 52, 54–55, 61, 63, 77-78, 84–85, 86–87, 89, 92, 100–102, 104–106
Voice and tone, 17–18, 57, 65, 72
VP, 54, 77

W

Webber, Emily, 105
Welfle, Andy, 24
Whiteboarding, 29, 61, 77
Wilkens, Jason, 94
Winters, Sarah, 8, 12, 14, 112
Wireframe, design, 93, 97
Word (Microsoft application), 40
Working Backwards, 46, 88
Workshop, hiring, 60–64, 65, 68, 78
Writer, in-house, 24–25
Writer (software application), 111, 119
Writing, v, 6, 8, 13, 14, 15, 23, 24-25, 36, 39, 40-42, 46-48, 56, 58, 62-63, 65, 72, 82, 84, 97, 98, 110-112, 115-117, 120

Y

YouTube, 42, 55, 118

Z

ZDNET, 12
Zipline, 4–5
Zo (chatbot), 115

ABOUT THE AUTHOR

Melanie Seibert has worked as a writer in tech for 25 years, having spent 6 of those years managing content and design teams. She built 2 content design teams from scratch and designed content for numerous digital products at companies like Rackspace, cPanel, Indeed, and PayPal.

She lives with her husband, 4 children, and their host of pets near Charlottesville, Virginia.

Printed in Dunstable, United Kingdom